Men-at-Arms • 536

# Renaissance Armies in Italy 1450–1550

Gabriele Esposito • Illustrated by Giuseppe Rava

Series editors Martin Windrow & Nick Reynolds

OSPREY PUBLISHING
Bloomsbury Publishing Plc

Kemp House, Chawley Park, Cumnor Hill, Oxford OX2 9PH, UK
29 Earlsfort Terrace, Dublin 2, Ireland
1385 Broadway, 5th Floor, New York, NY 10018, USA
Email: info@ospreypublishing.com
www.ospreypublishing.com

OSPREY is a trademark of Osprey Publishing Ltd

First published in Great Britain in 2020
Transferred to digital print in 2023

A catalogue record for this book is available from the British Library.

Print ISBN: 978 1 4728 4199 5
ePub: 978 1 4728 4200 8
ePDF: 978 1 4728 4197 1
XML: 978 1 4728 4198 8

Editor: Martin Windrow
Map by Wikimedia user 'Capmo'
Index by Rob Munro
Typeset by PDQ Digital Media Solutions, Bungay, UK
Printed and bound in India by Replika Press Private Ltd.

MIX
Paper from
responsible sources
FSC® C016779

24 25 26 27 28   10 9 8 7 6

**The Woodland Trust**
Osprey Publishing supports the Woodland Trust, the UK's leading woodland
conservation charity.

**www.ospreypublishing.com**
To find out more about our authors and books visit our website. Here you will
find extracts, author interviews, details of forthcoming events and the option
to sign-up for our newsletter.

## Dedication

To my parents Maria Rosario and Benedetto, for their immense love and help.
Thanks to them, I learned the real meaning of the word *Rinascimento*.

## Acknowledgements

As always, special thanks are due to the series editor Martin Windrow, for his
encouragement and advice; and to Giuseppe Rava, for the brilliantly colourful
plates that illustrate this title.
Most of the pictures published in this book were obtained from the Digital
Collections of the New York Public Library; the original files are available at:
https://digitalcollections.nypl.org/

## Artist's note

**OPPOSITE**
**A famous portrait of a *condottiero* made by Andrea del
Castagno in about 1450. This magnificent Florentine fresco
shows the appearance of a mercenary captain from the
middle decades of the 15th century, which was probably
essentially unchanged in the early 1500s. Note the details of
the brightly polished Milanese plate armour, over a ringmail
shirt visible at the upper arms and hip; the left pauldron is
asymmetrically large and reinforced with a rondel, since he
would not normally carry a shield. Both the soft *berretta* cap
and the quilted *sopravveste* worn over the armour are shown
in shades of red - an individual choice rather than livery. A
cap was sometimes worn as an alternative to the helmet
even in the field.**

# RENAISSANCE ARMIES IN ITALY 1450–1550

## INTRODUCTION

The Italian historical period commonly known as the Renaissance or 'Rebirth' coincided with the end of the medieval feudal system that had characterized most of Europe for centuries. In northern and central Italy particularly, wealthy merchant classes controlled cities that had already wrested independence from feudal overlords. Simultaneously, throughout large parts of the continent, the previously complete cultural dominance of the Roman Catholic Church was challenged by a new age of intellectual curiosity, partly based on a rebirth of interest in the achievements of the Classical world which was made possible by the spread of printing.

Alongside the consequent flowering of the arts came a new appetite for scientific enquiry, as educated men energetically explored the complexities of their world. Their efforts would advance every field

DOMINVS FARINATA DEVICTIS SVE PATRE LIBERATOR

of knowledge, including the arts of war. Because Italy was the arena for great-power struggles in the late 15th–early 16th centuries, both the 'infantry revolution' and the development of effective gunpowder weapons on the battlefield became particularly marked during the Italian Wars of the *Rinascimento*.

In any overview of military history, there are two dates that may be considered as marking the beginning and end of the Renaissance: 1453, and 1559. In 1453 France's Hundred Years' War with England ended with French unification (apart from the Duchy of Burgundy), into a monarchy with resources great enough to soon make it one of Europe's dominant military powers. In the same year, Constantinople and the last remnants of the Byzantine Empire were conquered by the Ottoman Turks. These two events had great consequences for Italy. The first marked the emergence of a threat to its northern borders, since France henceforward had the military potential to expand into the peninsula, lured by its wealth and fragmented politics. The second led to the arrival of a last flood of Byzantine immigrants carrying with them the heritage of Classical antiquity, increasing its already considerable effect on Italian culture. The perceived Ottoman menace also encouraged, in 1454, the conclusion of the Peace of Lodi, by which the major Italian states sought to establish political stability in the face of foreign threats. This brought a 40-year respite from the previously incessant regional wars, although the basic rivalries naturally persisted.

In 1494 this respite ended when, for the first time in many years, a foreign monarch invaded Italy with a great army: King Charles VIII of France (r. 1483–98). The arrival of the French destroyed any hope of Italian political stability, as other foreign powers joined a struggle for possession of the peninsula in the long and bloody Italian Wars. These saw the participation of all the significant Italian states in addition to that of France, a newly unified Spain, and the Holy Roman (essentially, Austro-German) Empire. Against the background of half a century of struggles between the French Valois dynasty and the Habsburg empire, a bewildering series of fragile coalitions were formed and broken; at one point France even allied itself with the Ottoman Turks against Imperial fellow Christians. In these campaigns armies made up of several different national contingents were the norm, and *condottieri* mercenary generals sometimes switched employers from season to season.

In 1559, the conclusion of the Peace of Cateau-Cambrésis brought the Italian Wars to an end: France had to renounce most of its expansionist ambitions, and Spain emerged as the dominant power in the peninsula. This coincided with exploitation of the resources of the New World, bringing far-reaching changes to the European balance of power. The Mediterranean became a secondary marketplace, while Europe turned its attentions to the Atlantic and beyond. The Italian states lost most of their political autonomy, becoming only minor participants in the new international order that was emerging.

# THE ITALIAN STATES

### The patterns of power, 14th–15th centuries

Since the 11th century the Italian peninsula had seen the rise of *comuni* (sing., *comune*) – rivalrous independent city-states that flourished through commerce, and were constantly at war with one another. Their autonomy grew during the 12th- and 13th-century struggles against the Holy Roman Empire, which formally claimed power over northern and central Italy. From the early 14th century, after many setbacks, the Emperors abandoned their claims over Italy; as a result, the *comuni* gradually became genuine states, entering a new phase of their history.

In southern Italy the situation was quite different: here the system of free *comuni* had never developed, and the whole region comprised a single state – the Kingdom of Naples. This was long ruled by foreign royal families, with (uniquely in Italy) a strong feudal nobility.

Between the *comuni* of the north and the feudal monarchy in the south there lay the central Papal States, where the Church in Rome had gradually created what was in effect a monarchy by acquiring power over neighbouring cities and provinces. This state had played a prominent role in the earlier struggle against the Holy Roman Empire, but during the 14th century it lost most of its political importance after, in 1309, the French-born Pope Clement V transferred his Holy See from Rome to Avignon in southern France.[1] Left leaderless, the Papal States entered a period of anarchy: most of the larger cities transformed themselves into free *comuni*, while the countryside came to be dominated by feudal lords. After Pope Gregory XI returned from Avignon to Rome in 1377, a reconquest of the Papal States was led by the Spanish cardinal Egidio Albornoz, who, at the head of a mercenary army, gradually subjugated all the polities that had emerged on the territory of the Papal States.

The beginning of the 15th century saw a gradual reduction of the extreme fragmentation of previous decades. In northern and central Italy the free *comuni* started to be transformed into larger local states known as *signorie* (sing., *signoria*). These were basically *comuni* where a prominent aristocratic or mercantile family had risen to a position of leadership. Initially, most of the *signorie* outwardly retained their republican forms of government; their *signori* saw no advantage in provoking popular resistance, so long as their practical control was not challenged. With the passage of time, the most important *signorie* started to absorb smaller neighbours, creating regional states around the most important city as capital.

In the south, meanwhile, the Angevin (French) royal family ruling the Kingdom of Naples was replaced after a bloody war by a new Aragonese (Spanish) dynasty in 1442. This had already controlled the island of Sicily since the end of the 13th century, and thus now unified two Italian kingdoms under one monarch (hence the later 'Kingdom of the Two Sicilies').

## Italy following the Treaty of Lodi, 1454

With the Treaty of Lodi, Italy entered a new settlement that remained mostly unchanged until the end of the Renaissance. This political geography was based on five main regional states: in the north, the Duchy of Milan and the Republic of Venice; in central Italy, the Papal States and the Republic of Florence; and in the south, the Kingdom of Naples.

The Duchy of Milan emerged as one of the most important military powers during the second half of the 15th century, absorbing all the other *signorie* of Lombardy. The Visconti family, which had formally established the duchy in 1395, continued to rule until 1447; three years later, after a brief period of republican government, the Sforza family (previously mercenary commanders under the Visconti) seized power.

The Republic of Venice had always enjoyed a great degree of autonomy from the Holy Roman Empire. Maritime commerce was the key to Venice's success, and the city had the peninsula's most important fleet. As one of the *comuni*, Venice gradually expanded its territory both in north-east Italy and also towards the Balkan coast of the Adriatic Sea. By the beginning of the 14th century the Venetians had already conquered large parts of Dalmatia (present-day Croatia), and were expanding into

Biftor Pisani. Admiral der Venezianer. Edelknappe.

A reconstruction of a mercenary captain (left) with his servant. Both wear the stiff *berretta* made of felt, here shown as red. The *condottiero* has complete armour, while his *paggio* has only half-armour. While the captain's over-armour garment is also shown as red, its heft and buckled fastenings indicate that it is protective. While the artist has omitted any external rivet-heads, it otherwise resembles a brigandine shown in a painting from the 1490s; the layering of plate, brigandine and mail defences was characteristic of the period.

---

1   Successive French-born popes would remain there until 1376, subject to manipulation in the political interests of French kings. Even after Gregory XI returned to Rome in January 1377, two more rival 'anti-popes' would contest his legitimacy from Avignon, and the schism would not finally be healed until 1417.

the Aegean Sea to occupy some spoils of the former Byzantine Empire. During the first half of the 15th century Milan and Venice fought several wars for dominance over northern Italy; this struggle ended with the Peace of Lodi, which gave north-west Italy to Milan and the north-east to Venice. Venice was formally an oligarchic republic, led by a *doge* (duke) elected by the most prominent merchant citizens.

In addition to Milan and Venice, there were another two regionally important states in the north: the Republic of Genoa, and the Duchy of Savoy. Genoa was Venice's main maritime rival; however, during the 15th century it was briefly occupied on a number of occasions by either France or Milan. The Duchy of Savoy, recognized as such in 1416, was a large feudal state located on the western borders of northern Italy; culturally, it had much more in common with France than with the rest of Italy. After the unification of the Kingdom of France in 1453 Savoy became a vassal state of the French, and would regain its full independence only with the Peace of Cateau-Cambrésis in 1559.

Together with Milan, Florence had been the most important of all the Italian *comuni*. From 1415–20 the city began to be dominated by the Medici family, owners of the richest and most flourishing bank in Europe. This dominated the economic life of Italy, and could influence the politics of foreign nations through manipulation of its loans. Cosimo de' Medici the Elder (1389–1464) and his family gradually assumed control of the Florentine Republic by ensuring their election to the most prominent offices of state.

The Papal States continued to expand during most of the Renaissance; during the latter period various popes acted as actual monarchs, and it was not unknown to see them in full armour at the head of their armies. Exploiting its religious authority, the Papacy sought to expand towards both Tuscany (dominated by Florence) and the southern territories of the Venetian Republic. The popes were absolute monarchs, who were elected by the cardinals. When the Spanish Borgia family tried to transform the Church into a dynastic monarchy, most of Italy turned against them to maintain the status quo.

The Kingdom of Naples, in southern Italy, had the largest army in the peninsula. Its Aragonese royal dynasty was politically independent from the branch of the family which ruled the Kingdom of Aragon in Spain, but formed part of the Aragonese commercial empire embracing several regions in the Mediterranean (such as Sardinia). In 1458, after 14 years of unification with the Kingdom of Naples under the same monarch, the Kingdom of Sicily regained its formal independence and returned under the direct rule of the Kingdom of Aragon. As a result, Sicily was not involved in the important political events of the Italian Wars, while the Kingdom of Naples was one of the main protagonists.

### The *Condottieri*

In the 14th-century *comuni*, service in the urban militias of disciplined infantry had offered the lower and middle classes opportunities for social advancement. While there were exceptions, it is broadly true to say that once they had achieved the status of merchants or well-to-do artisans, this wealthier *borghesia* tended to prefer paying for others to protect their communities. Thus, the 15th-century *signorie* increasingly relied upon employed companies of mercenary soldiers – initially mostly foreigners but, as time passed, also other Italians.

These *compagnie di ventura* might number anything from a few hundred to several thousand professional soldiers, each company being commanded by a *capitano di ventura* – usually a younger son of an aristocratic family – who was responsible for its recruiting and administration. Such mercenary captains negotiated contracts (*condotte* – sing., *condotta*) with the civil authorities of the various *signorie*. As a result, the companies themselves came to be known as *condotte* and their captains as *condottieri* ('contractors' – sing., *condottiero*). Frequently a *condotta* represented virtually the whole army of a *signoria*; inevitably, that state then found itself a hostage to the ambitions of a warlord who might decide to change sides, or to simply seize power for himself (as the Sforza did, after the Visconti were deposed in Milan). Before the 1490s battles were seldom costly in lives, usually being fought between fellow professionals to obtain field advantage and capture wealthy prisoners for ransom. The only way to ensure the loyalty of mercenary commanders was to pay them ever-increasing sums, with the result that most Renaissance Italian states were always on the verge of bankruptcy. The degeneration of this military system led Italy into a state of anarchy, with mercenary armies raiding and looting at will. Under mercenary generals, the expanded *condotte* continued to form important parts of even the foreign armies engaged in Italy during the 16th-century wars.

Organizationally, a mercenary company's basic tactical building-block was a *lancia* ('lance', pl. *lance*) of three men and five horses. The first man, or *elmetto* ('helmet'), was a fully armoured man-at-arms or knight; the second was a *scudiero* ('squire') equipped as a light cavalryman; and the third, a *paggio* ('page'), acting both as a servant and as an infantryman in battle. Two of the five horses were *destieri*, high-quality warhorses for the man-at-arms; two were lesser-quality *ronzini* used by the squire; and the last was a pack-horse for the page. The 'lances' within a *condotta* could be assembled into larger sub-units for specific purposes or to fight in a pitched battle. Five 'lances' made up a *posta* of 15 men, or ten an *insegna* of 30; five *poste* made up a *bandiera* of 75; and 20–30 'lances' might be assembled into a *squadra* of 60–90 men – the largest component within a *condotta*, commanded by a *squadriere* or junior captain serving at the orders of the commander.

In countries such as France and Burgundy, the tactical 'lance' included two additional specialist infantrymen – archers or crossbowmen (or latterly, arquebusiers with handguns). This five-man model never became popular in Italy, where contingents of specialized infantry always remained distinct components of the various armies. From 1464 the Papal army did start to deploy the five-man *corazza* ('cuirass', pl. *corazze*) with one man-at-arms, two squires and two pages, but this remained a local experiment. Each Italian army of the period also included a

Impression of an Italian heavy cavalryman of the mid-16th century; the elaborate plumes on the visored armet helmet and the horse's richly embroidered *bardatura* suggest a ceremonial occasion rather than the battlefield. The Italian Wars may be seen as the high point of this fully developed knightly battle-armour, but also as its swansong.

An impression of Italian infantrymen from the last decades of the 15th century; the artist was no student of armour, but the overall silhouettes seem fairly realistic. The oval shield (left) was carried by the majority of Italian heavy infantry, as also was plate arm and leg armour in combination with mail shirts, and the short cape is characteristically Italian. The billman is illustrated as wearing brigandine protection over mail; the continuation of the internal riveted plates over the arms seems unlikely and ringmail sleeves would be more convincing. Infantry helmets were basically sallets, but of a wide range of shapes.

certain number of men-at-arms who served individually with their 'lances' and not as part of a *condotta*, these *lance spezzate* ('broken lances') were often former members of a *condotta* that had been disbanded. On occasion, numbers of these might be gathered by a captain to form a new *condotta*.

The contracts signed between *condottieri* and their employers (either communities or individuals) were quite sophisticated, covering not only numbers and types of troops, pay, length of service, provisions, etc., but also aspects such as tax and toll exemptions for the mercenaries, discipline and inspections, punishments for desertion or betrayal, and more. The period of service for a company initially lasted only three or six months. Later it was increased to 12 months, divided into two phases: the first six months of *ferma* or active service, which could be expanded at need by a further six months *de rispetto* – a sort of reserve service, during which the company had to remain at the disposal of its employer. In peacetime, an alternative *condotta di aspetto* prescribed a period on half or one-third pay, during which the *condottiero* undertook to keep his men available for service in case of need.

Initially, this kind of contract was not particularly popular, but, since a *condottiero* might actually exploit it by fighting for a second employer while still being in reserve for the first, such retaining contracts became more common. As time passed, an increasing number of mercenary commanders started to sign longer-term contracts with Italian states, so that large bodies of mercenaries gradually became transformed into relatively stable standing armies serving a single *signoria*. During the final period of the Renaissance, all Italian armies started to include an increasing number of standing military units (*provvisione*) receiving fixed pay on a regular basis. These *provvisionati* soldiers, who usually made up the personal guards of rulers or acted as garrison troops, had better equipment and training than most of the average shorter-term *condotte*, although several of the latter already had some permanent elements. The most important *condottieri* each had their own *casa* or 'household', comprising a marshal, chancellors, cooks, chaplains, musicians and a mounted escort.

A handicap for the Italian states when they were invaded by foreign armies of more balanced composition was the fact that the mercenary armies of the *signorie* were mostly made up of heavy cavalry, with infantry in only an auxiliary role. Consequently, most *signorie* continued to field some contingents of urban militia during the Renaissance period; while these infantrymen were initially poorly trained and equipped, they could be called up in great numbers in times of emergency. Over time, the militia systems of all the Italian states were reformed and expanded in order to meet the new threats represented by foreign armies. Their quality improved considerably, but they remained a secondary element, and never reached the same standards as the foreign professional footsoldiers.

As regards light cavalry, in addition to the *scudieri* integral to the 'lances', Italian armies of the period did include some other contingents, usually from outside Italy. The Republic of Venice could count on the excellent *stradiotti* from the Balkans, and the Kingdom of Naples on Albanian light horsemen.

# CHRONOLOGY

Names of major battles are printed in **bold**. Simultaneous events outside Italy are printed (*in parentheses and italics*).

**1454:** Conclusion of the Peace of Lodi; this recognizes the Sforza as rulers of Milan, and settles the mutual status of Milan, Venice, the Papal States, Florence, and the Kingdom of Naples.

**1458:** France occupies Genoa for the first time. Ferrante (Ferdinand) I is crowned King of Naples, thus ending the personal union with the Kingdom of Sicily, which remains under the control of Aragon.

**1467:** Venice tries to depose the Medici family, rulers of Florence, by supporting the rival Soderini. In July, a 14,000-strong Venetian mercenary army led by *condottiero* Bartolomeo Collona is checked at Riccardina (Molinella), by a comparable Florentine-Milanese force commanded by *condottiero* Federico da Montefeltro. Losses are modest, despite significant use of artillery and handguns.

**1469:** After death of his father Piero, Lorenzo de' Medici (later 'the Magnificent') rules Florence together with his younger brother Giuliano. (*Marriage between Ferdinand II of Aragon and Isabel of Castile begins unification of most of Spain.*)

**1478:** Pope Sixtus V is party to a plot to depose the Medici in Florence. This 'Pazzi conspiracy' leads to the assassination of Giuliano de' Medici; Lorenzo survives, and has most of the conspirators killed.

At **Giornico** in December, small rearguard of a Swiss army that had besieged Bellinzona uses mountain terrain and snowy conditions to humiliatingly defeat a much larger Milanese force.

**1480–81:** Ottoman fleet invades Kingdom of Naples, and in August 1480 occupies coastal city of Otranto. Christian forces under King Ferdinand I of Naples besiege city in May 1481, and Turks – unsupported since death of Sultan Mehmet that month – surrender in September.

**1482–84:** 'War of Ferrara' for control of that city, between alliances of Papal States–Venice on one side and Kingdom of Naples–Florence on the other. War ends indecisively, with Venice gaining some territory but Ferrara still independent.

**1485:** Kingdom of Naples ravaged by internal 'Conspiracy of the Barons' against Aragonese monarchy, but King Ferdinand I crushes feudal aristocracy with his paid professional troops.

**1492:** In Florence, Lorenzo de' Medici dies and is succeeded by his son Piero. The Spanish Cardinal Rodrigo Borgia becomes Pope Alexander VI. (*Capture of Granada, final Moorish possession in southern Spain, by combined armies of Aragon and Castile.*

*Columbus lands in the Americas while seeking a western route to India.*)

**1494:** Outbreak of Italian Wars: on death of Ferdinand I of Naples, Charles VIII of France claims that throne, invading Italy with a large army, with agreement of Duke Ludovico Sforza of Milan. Piero de' Medici, fearing conquest of Florence, allows the French army to cross Tuscany and cedes some castles. This provokes popular revolt: the Medicis are forced to flee, and Florentine republic comes under theocratic leadership of fundamentalist monk Girolamo Savonarola.

**1495:** Charles VIII easily conquers Kingdom of Naples, whose King Ferdinand II withdraws to Sicily, where he is supported by Ferdinand II of Spain and Sicily. Anti-French 'Holy League' formed by Naples, Sicily, Venice, Milan, the Papal States, the Holy Roman Empire, and (peripherally) England. Charles VIII, isolated in southern Italy, defeats a Neapolitan-Spanish army at **Seminara** in June, demonstrating superiority of French cavalry and Swiss pikemen, but soon afterwards loses Naples. Marching north to return to France, Charles meets a Venetian-Milanese army led by Francesco Gonzaga at **Fornovo**, near Parma, in July. Fought in rainy weather, the battle is indecisive; the League suffers heavier casualties, and Charles continues his march north, but has to abandon all his artillery and accumulated loot.

The Aragonese King Ferdinand II retakes the throne of Naples.

**1497:** French – Spanish clashes in Roussillon, southern France.

**1498:** Popular revolt in Florence leads to deposition and later execution of Savonarola.

**1499:** (*Emperor Maximilian I unsuccessfully invades Swiss cantons; after his defeat at **Dornach** in July, subsequent Peace of Basle formally recognizes Swiss independence from Austria.*)

King Louis XII of France leads second invasion of Italy with army including large number of Swiss mercenaries. He takes Milan, driving Ludovico Sforza into exile and ending Milan's

| Marquisate of Saluzzo | Marquisate of Montferrat | Bishopric of Trent | Marquisate of Mantua | Republic of Lucca | Duchies of Modena & Ferrara |

Duchy of Savoy

Duchy of Milan

Republic of Venice

Austria

Hungary

Republic of Genoa

Republic of Florence

San Marino

Venetian Dalmatia

Ottoman Empire

Corsica (Genoa)

Republic of Siena

Papal States

Kingdom of Naples

Republic of Ragusa

Sardinia (Aragon)

Rome
Pontecorvo
Benevento
Naples

**Italy**
**1494**

Palermo

Kingdom of Sicily (Aragon)

Syracuse

Sketch map showing the five major regional states at the outbreak of the Italian Wars (Milan, Venice, Florence, the Papal States, and the Kingdom of Naples), with their neighbours and satellites. (CC BY-SA 3.0, Wikimedia user 'Capmo')

independence. French march south into Romagna, with support of Pope Alexander VI, who hopes for creation of a northern Italian possession for his son Cesare Borgia.

**1500:** Achieving little in Romagna, Louis XII marches south for Naples. At this date both France and Spain seek elimination of independent Aragonese Neapolitan monarchy, so conclude short-lived secret Treaty of Granada to divide Kingdom of Naples between them.

**1503:** Outbreak of hostilities between France and Spain for possession of Kingdom of Naples. At **Cerignola** near Bari, in April, a Spanish-Landsknecht-Italian army led by Gonzalo Fernández de Córdoba defeats stronger French-Swiss army led by Duke of Nemours; cannon and entrenched Spanish arquebusiers break both French cavalry and Swiss infantry attacks, inflicting some 4,000 deaths (including Nemours) for only about 500 Spanish.

In December, Córdoba again defeats a French army at the **Garigliano** river, near Gaeta, by means of a surprise crossing. By these two decisive victories, Spain secures dominance over the Kingdom of Naples for centuries thereafter. Pope Alexander VI dies, succeeded by Julius II, of the Della Rovere family.

**1504:** Armistice of Lyon brings Franco-Spanish hostilities to an end, with France annexing Duchy of Milan and Spain retaining Kingdom of Naples.

**1508:** Emperor Maximilian I organizes anti-Venetian alliance ('League of Cambrai') with France, Spain and Papal States. His main object is to expand Imperial territories in north-eastern Italy at the expense of Venice.

**1509:** In May, Venetian mercenary rearguard force, led by Bartolomeo Orsini d'Alviano, is defeated at **Agnadello (Vaila)** by larger French-Swiss army under King Louis XII.

**1511:** League of Cambrai is dissolved, when Pope Julius II decides to form new alliance to expel the French from Italy. This new 'Holy League' includes the Papal States, Venice, Spain, and Swiss cantons.

**Near-contemporary engraving from a drawing by Hans Holbein, giving a realistic idea of the clash of two pike blocks during a Renaissance battle. In the foreground, 'double-pay soldiers' armed with halberds and two-handed swords seem to be coming forward up a flank from their original positions in the rear ranks. The soldiers on both sides fought with much the same weapons, so when pike blocks came together it was usually only differences in discipline or morale that decided the outcome. The majority of the killing took place only after one formation had begun to collapse and give way.**

The two major innovations that brought an end to the supremacy of both the armoured knight, and the unsupported Swiss pike block: the arquebus, and the field-artillery cannon. This arquebusier and gunner are identified as belonging to the French army of Francis 1, who employed many German mercenaries for his 1515 campaign. The Emperor Maximilian I acquired bored-out cast-bronze guns, and organized German artillery to at least reduce the previous complete lack of standardization. It is still hard to interpret the various categories: this heavy field piece might be a *Kartaune*, with a barrel length up to 8½ times its calibre.

**1512:** In April, French-Italian-Landsknecht army in Lombardy, led by Gaston de Foix, wins great victory at **Ravenna** over Holy League army of Spanish and Papal troops under Ramón de Cardonna. First known example of long preliminary duel between each sides' field artillery, inflicting heavy losses before armies clash. French win cavalry encounters; Spanish infantry at first repulse Gascon crossbowmen and Landsknechts, until overwhelmed from all sides by French cavalry, but Gaston de Foix is killed.

However, large Swiss reinforcements soon arrive for the League; the French are obliged to abandon Milan, and withdraw from Italy during summer. Swiss mercenaries restore Maximilian Sforza (briefly) as Duke of Milan, and the Medici return to power in Florence.

**1513:** Pope Julius II dies and is succeeded by Leo X, of the Medici family. Venice abandons the Holy League and changes sides. In June, French-Landsknecht army led by Louis de la Trémoille is defeated at **Novara** by mostly Swiss army fighting for Milan; Swiss capture French baggage and guns, execute Landsknecht prisoners and pursue French as far as Dijon.

*(In August, during separate campaign between Holy Roman Empire and France, Emperor Maximilian I and King Henry VIII of England defeat French army under Jacques de la Palice at Guinegatte in Artois – 'Battle of the Spurs'.)*

**1515:** Shortly after his accession, King Francis I of France invades Lombardy. He takes 72 cannon over Alpine passes, and a daring pre-emptive raid effectively knocks the Papal States and Spain out of the war by capturing the Papal commander, Prospero Colonna.

In September, at **Marignano** near Milan, 32,000 French and a few Venetians, deployed in all-arms divisions behind massed artillery guarded by Landsknechts, eventually win a hard-fought evening-and-morning battle against 22,000 unsupported Swiss pikemen. France recovers Duchy of Milan, and Holy League ceases to exist.

**1516:** Treaty of Noyon confirms division of Italy into two spheres of influence: that of the Duchy of Milan under French control, and the Kingdom of Naples dominated by Spain.

Under Treaty of Friburg with France, the Swiss cantons renounce their expansionist ambitions in Italy and become neutral, although individual Swiss mercenary bands will still seek employment.

*(King Charles I of Habsburg dynasty succeeds to the throne of Spain.)*

**1519:** *(Charles I becomes Holy Roman Emperor Charles V. This unification of Spain and the Empire under his personal control will be intolerable to France.)*

*1521:* *(New war breaks out between France and Spain; French invade Luxembourg in Low Countries, and Navarre in Spain.)*

*(Protestant preacher Martin Luther is excommunicated by Pope Leo X. At the Diet of Worms, spokesmen for Emperor Charles V condemn doctrines expounded by Luther.)*

In November, French lose Milan to surprise attack by Imperial-Spanish-Papal army under Prospero Colonna.

**1522:** In April, French-Venetian-Swiss army under Odet de Lautrec is defeated at **Bicocca river** by Colonna's smaller Imperial-Spanish army fighting on defensive; impatient attack by unpaid Swiss mercenaries, who outpace French artillery, is bloodily defeated by Spanish arquebusiers. Days later, Swiss leave Italy.

**1523:** Venice makes peace with Emperor; French withdraw from Italy.

**1524:** In August, Lannoy's Imperial-Spanish army defeats a French-Swiss force under Guillaume Goufier de Bonnivet at the **Sesia river**; French forced to abandon Milan yet again, and Imperial army briefly invades Provence.

In October, King Francis I leads 40,000 men back into Lombardy and besieges city of Pavia. (Meanwhile, the Empire is distracted by the internal German Peasants' War.)

**1525:** In February, Emperor Charles V sends 22,000 Imperial-Spanish troops under Lannoy to break siege of **Pavia**; his 12,000 Landsknechts, 5,000 Spanish and 3,000 Italian infantry are commanded by mercenary generals Pescara and Frundsberg. Francis's infantry include 8,000 Swiss and 9,000 German and Italian mercenaries. In a confused battle between separated forces fighting with little coordination, the French cavalry are defeated and destroyed by Imperial infantry. French casualties are about 8,000, including many nobles killed, and King Francis wounded and captured, against perhaps 1,000 Imperial casualties. Observers note Swiss lack of aggressive confidence since their losses at the Bicocca.

**1526:** Following the battle of Pavia, France forms anti-Imperial 'League of Cognac' with Venice, Genoa, the Papal States and Florence.

**1527:** Imperial Landsknechts occupy and sack Rome. Meanwhile, the Medici family is expelled from Florence once again, and a new republic is proclaimed. The French conquer Genoa and then move south, laying siege to city of Naples without success.

**1528:** In order to restore the Medici to power in Florence, Charles V's Imperial army besieges the city.

(*Victories in Balkans allow Ottoman Turks to advance as far as Vienna, which they besiege without success.*)

**1529:** Peace of Cambrai ends second war between Charles V and Francis I. France cedes Duchy of Milan to Spain, but receives Duchy of Burgundy from the Empire.

French artillerymen loading what may be one of several medium types of gun variously termed culverins or 'sows'. The gunners, in civilian clothing, are probably well-paid specialists hired on temporary contract; in one 16th-century Imperial army even the loaders were paid one-third more than common Landsknechts. Given the huge costs, most field armies seem to have had only 20–30 guns. Though considered the best in Europe, the French artillery had few occasions to distinguish itself in open battle. An exception was the 1515 campaign, when King Francis I managed to take 72 cannon south over the Alpine passes – an enormous undertaking, which must have needed several thousand horses and hundreds of wagons. At Marignano the French guns proved effective, but since they were positioned forward of the infantry they had to be guarded by a selected body of Landsknechts (the notorious 'Black Band'); nevertheless, Swiss pikemen did briefly manage to capture some cannon.

**1530:** After a long siege, Florence is occupied by Imperial forces; republican government is replaced by the restored Medici.

**1531:** (*Protestant princes in Germany form 'Schmalkaldic League' against Emperor Charles V.*)

**1536–38:** Emperor Charles V inherits rule of Milan through his daughter, widow of childless Francesco Sforza. Third Valois–Habsburg war breaks out. After concluding an alliance with Ottoman Turks, France occupies Duchy of Savoy as preliminary to invasion of Lombardy. Imperial armies invade Provence and Picardy, but campaigns end in stalemate. Joint French-Ottoman fleet attacks Genoa, but is repulsed with heavy losses.

**1538:** Truce of Nice between France and Empire, ostensibly intended to last ten years.

**1542:** Fourth Valois–Habsburg war breaks out; inconclusive fighting in Roussillon, and northern Italy.

**1543:** Franco-Ottoman fleet captures Nice from Imperial garrison. Inconclusive Imperial and French manoeuvring in Picardy.

Near-contemporary representation of the battle of Pavia (1525), showing some of the Landsknechts who, alongside Spanish infantry, played an important role in the Emperor's victory. It was a confused engagement, which began with a surprise advance by night that caught the French army wrongly aligned; continued with a sortie by a besieged Imperial garrison that caught them between two fires; and ended with the French cavalry confined between woods and surrounded by well-orchestrated infantry units of 'pike and shot'. Pavia is judged by many to have set the final seal on the Renaissance 'infantry revolution'.

**1544:** In April, at **Ceresole** south of Turin, French-Swiss-Italian army under Prince d'Enghien narrowly defeats Imperial-Spanish-Italian army of Marqués del Vasco; heavy losses on both sides.

**1546:** *(Schmalkaldic War breaks out in Germany, between Protestant princes and Emperor.)*

**1547:** *(Imperial army led by Duke of Alba, and including Spanish tercios, wins decisive battle of Muhlberg against Schmalkaldic League.)*
King Francis I dies, and is succeeded on French throne by his son Henry II.

**1551:** Henry II of France concludes alliance with the most important Lutheran princes of Germany. Renewal of hostilities between France and the Empire/Spain.

**1554:** With Imperial support, Cosimo I de' Medici attacks Florence's last Tuscan rival, Republic of Siena. In August, at battle of **Scannagallo (Marciano)**, mixed Florentine-Spanish army under Gian Giacomo Medici defeats Sienese-French army of Piero Strozzi.

**1555:** In April, city of Siena finally surrenders (republic will be incorporated into Duchy of Florence in 1559).

*(In September, Peace of Augsburg finally brings hostilities between Charles V and German Protestant principalities to an end; princes recognize Emperor's authority, but are free to choose their desired form of Christianity.)*

**1556:** *(After a lifetime of war, the ailing Charles V abdicates, dividing his immense territorial possessions: his son Philip II inherits the Kingdom of Spain, its Italian dominions, Flanders, and the American colonies; as Emperor, Charles's brother Ferdinand I will reign over the Austro-German heartland, Bohemia and Hungary.)*

**1557:** In August, at St Quentin in Flanders, King Philip's Spanish army led by the Duke of Savoy (with minor support from English troops) defeats a French relief force under Gonzaga and Montmorency.

**1559:** The Peace of Cateau-Cambrésis definitively ends the Italian Wars. France renounces all its claims in Italy; the Duchy of Savoy is restored as an independent state; and most of Italy remains under Spanish control. The Italian states have forever lost their independence, and large parts of the peninsula (Duchy of Milan, Kingdom of Naples, Kingdom of Sicily, plus Sardinia) are occupied by Spanish troops.

# THE ARMIES:

## DUCHY OF MILAN

During the second half of the 15th century, the Milanese army led by members of the Sforza family was (along with that of Naples) the largest Italian military force, and enjoyed an excellent reputation for its high level of professionalism. Unlike other state forces, it included a good number of standing *provvisionati* units, as well as a strong ducal household contingent (*famiglia ducale*). In 1462 the army comprised 3,500 three-man 'lances', for a total of 11,500 soldiers. Of these, 2,625 'lances' (7,875 men) were members of *condotte*, and 875 (2,625) were *lance spezzate*. In addition to the above, there were also 1,200 infantrymen in various mercenary companies in the service of the duke.

### 'Broken lances'

Initially the *lance spezzate* were rarely employed as an independent corps on the battlefield, being mostly used to replace casualties or deserters in the standard 'lance'. Later, around 1468, the 'broken lances' were organized into three autonomous units: the *lancie spezzate che sono in ordine* ('ordered broken lances'); the *lancie spezzate che non sono in ordine* ('disordered broken lances'); and the *lancie spezzate di nuovi condottieri* ('broken lances of new *condottieri*'). The first of these corps comprised three-man 'lances'; the second, nominal 'lances' with only one or two men; and the third, the 'lances' of minor mercenary captains who had only recently been employed. Later still, all the 'broken lances' were assembled into a single corps of 2,500 men – a tendency that had become common during recent decades. It was encouraged by the fact that these individuals generally proved more loyal to their employers than those already assembled under the command of a *condottiero* to whom they owed their paid obedience.

### Ducal household

Originally organized under the Visconti, this comprised professional knights who served with their personal 'lances' at the direct orders of the duke, most being members of the duke's family or men otherwise strongly linked to his interests. In 1462 the household had 328 three-man 'lances', totalling 954 fighting men; some years later it was expanded to 400 'lances', of which 100 made up the duke's mounted escort; but by the end of the 15th century, shortly before the French invasion of Milan, it had been reduced to just 200 'lances'.

These extremely loyal *famigliari armigeri* men-at-arms were considered to be among the best heavy cavalrymen in Italy, particularly after the Sforza dukes improved their equipment and training. Both the 'family at arms' and the 'broken lances' received higher pay than the common mercenaries, quarters, and occasional bonuses. In addition to the heavy cavalry the ducal household included a light-cavalry corps of *galuppi* – young probationers from the leading families of Lombardy, who got chances to demonstrate their courage in battle in hope of being promoted to the status of men-at-arms. They

Approximate artist's impression of a heavy cavalryman in full armour, with a 'close helmet' or armet, and a heavy lance swollen out to protect the handgrip. Milan was the major centre of armour production in Italy, and its products were exported and copied throughout Europe. The duchy's own heavy cavalry was composed of the strong household contingent of the Sforza dukes, three-man 'lances' in hired *condotte*, and, from the 1470s, individuals from 'broken lances' assembled into a single corps paid by the dukes. From 1494 onwards, Milan was the first objective of repeated French invasions of Lombardy.

also performed 'police' duties – patrolling the extensive countryside of Lombardy, preventing smuggling along the lengthy border with the Republic of Venice, and clearing the streets of Milan of rebels at times of popular unrest.

### Regularly paid troops

The Milanese *provvisionati* were mostly infantrymen, paid by the central administration. In time of war they had no great value, but in peacetime they formed an effective security force. Their numbers fluctuated during the second half of the 15th century; at their peak there were 4,000, but they were later greatly reduced. Those who provided the city garrison of Milan enjoyed better pay and conditions than those stationed in other areas of the duchy; 200 of them made up the garrison of the Castello Sforzesco, the city's main fortification. Over time, the infantry payroll began to include a certain number of foreigners (mostly Germans) of absolute loyalty to the duke, who were equipped with early firearms.

Alongside the *galuppi*, for maintaining law and order in the countryside and guarding the border the Dukes of Milan employed two 150-man squadrons of paid *balestrieri a cavallo* (mounted crossbowmen), who were highly mobile and effective professionals. Unlike mounted crossbowmen of the previous period, these were not 'mounted infantry', but actually used their weapons from the saddle with notable skill.

### Common militia

Theoretically, the Milanese army could also call upon local militias known as *Cernide*, comprising all able-bodied citizens of the duchy. In fact, they had never been called up since the early decades of the 15th century; by 1450 their organization had deteriorated, and thereafter some were raised only for brief periods during military emergencies. The rural *Cernide*, however, frequently provided good numbers of auxiliary non-combatants to assist during military campaigns. These peasants proved to be good sappers, and were also employed to transport heavy equipment, including that of the artillery. In 1469 the *Cernide* were reorganized for the last time, receiving a new structure including 9,000 infantrymen and 1,260 non-combatant *guastatori* sappers.

### REPUBLIC OF VENICE

The city of Venice was the most important of the 'maritime republics', which were free *comuni* that had created commercial empires in the Mediterranean thanks to the size and skill of their fleets. Venice was ruled by a Council of the Ten, an oligarchic assembly that elected from among its number the presiding *doge* or duke. By the beginning of the 15th century, Genoa, Venice's only serious rival, had been much weakened by wars with France and Milan, leaving Venice unchallenged. The republic could therefore expand its dominions in north-east Italy, replacing Padua as the local regional power, and in the Adriatic Sea, on the Balkan coastline of Dalmatia. In the latter region, by the mid-15th century the Venetians had several important bases and were recruiting a good number of their troops. Consequently, Venetian forces were formally divided between the *Terraferma* (the Italian territories) and the troops recruited from the *Stato da Mar* (the overseas territories).

## Infantry pre-1509

This category included a number of small 'guard' units, which served in the city of Venice under the orders of the Council of the Ten as a combination militarized police force and fire-brigade. These 630 chosen soldiers were distributed as follows: 30 formed the garrison of the Doge's palace; 100 patrolled the lagoon and the city's canals in small boats; 200, selected by the leaders of the six neighbourhoods (the *Sestieri*) that formed the city, garrisoned the Piazza San Marco in the commercial heart of Venice; and 300 provided ten-man patrols for each of the city's 30 parishes. These guardsmen were collectively known as *Arsenalotti*, since most of them were also craftsmen working in the famous naval and military Arsenal.

The immediately available Venetian infantry were a body totalling 9,000 soldiers, to which each of the city's six neighbourhoods was to provide 1,500 men. These were a sort of semi-professional militiamen, who had to be ready at all times to turn out in case of emergencies. If Venice were to be attacked, half of the 9,000 would assemble in the Piazza San Marco while the others remained dispersed to protect their home *Sestiere*. These 9,000 militiamen always remained in the *Terraferma*, and had a purely defensive role.

This force was chosen from among the general militia, which could muster a total of 40,000 infantrymen. Every able-bodied male citizen aged 20–60 was legally obliged to serve in case of need. The militia was organized in 12-man squads known as *duodene*; of these 12, in peacetime only one man, chosen by lot, had to serve at any one time. In time of war, two or sometimes even three men of each *duoderna* might be called up. These 3,000–6,000 'standard' militiamen serving at any one time were mostly employed in the *Stato da Mar*, their primary task being to provide the necessary embarked naval infantry contingents for the large Venetian fleet.

In 1477 the government decided to reform its armed forces following the example of the Milanese *provvisionati*, and united the 9,000 semi-permanent militiamen and the 3,000–6,000 'standard' militiamen into a single body of full-time paid soldiers known as *provvisionati di San Marco*. The 12,000–15,000 men of this new corps were the largest and best professional infantry force in Italy.

## Infantry post-1509

In 1509 the general organization of the Venetian infantry was completely changed, due to the military emergency facing the republic during that crucial year of French victories. It was decided to expand the militia system over the rural territories of all the republic's cities, by recruiting all able-bodied men aged 16–40. The contribution of the rural areas proved to be significant, with 9,000 militiamen recruited in a short time for the campaign of 1509. The new rural militia units were known as *Cernide*.

In 1528 these were completely reorganized, reaching an impressive establishment of 20,000 infantry organized in companies of 500–800 each. In case of foreign invasion the *Cernide* were to defend the main fortifications in their home territories, and for this reason they were equipped from the start with early forms of firearms. Soon after the

Identified as a knight of the French *Compagnies d'Ordonnance*, this image seems to depict Milanese armour of *c.*1515–30. The heavy plate horse-armour naturally reduced the destrier's mobility and endurance, and muddy conditions might also hamper the heavy cavalry more than flanking bodies of light horse, as at Fornovo in 1495.

**17**

introduction of this new *Cernide* system, rural militias of the same kind were also organized in the Venetian territories of the *Stato da Mar*; these differed only in being known as *Craine*.

In 1550 the soldiers serving on Venetian warships were separated from the rest of the militia to form a permanent professional corps of naval infantry, *fanti da mar*. The latter included Balkan subjects of Venice recruited from the Slavic populations of Dalmatia, and known as *schiavoni* or *oltremarini*. Generally speaking, the new Venetian militias organized during the first half of the 16th century were not of the highest quality, except for those coming from the mountain territories of Friuli, where there was a long historic tradition of effective peasant militias.

## Cavalry

The cavalry of the *Terraferma* consisted entirely of mercenary 'lances' and 'broken lances', since Venice had never enjoyed much of a cavalry tradition. A variable number around 1,000 'lances' were usually kept on permanent service, while others were employed only in time of war and according to circumstances. Initially the 'broken lances' made up a good proportion of Venice's mercenary cavalry, but by 1500 they had mostly been absorbed into the standard units.

As throughout Italy, the Venetian 'lance' initially comprised three men, of whom the squire was here termed an *utile*. Over time, however, a fourth man (1490) and then a fifth (1494) were added to each *lancia*. These were usually mounted crossbowmen, but might also be mounted handgunners – mostly German mercenaries, since firearms were not yet plentiful in Italy. With the expansion to five men the Venetian 'lances' started to be known as 'cuirasses'. The mercenary companies of the *condottieri*, as in the rest of Italy, also included small contingents of well-trained infantrymen.

The overseas territories of the *Stato da Mar* did provide some Albanian and Cretan light infantry, but their main contribution to the Venetian forces was the famous *stradiotti* light cavalry. The great majority of these were Balkan mercenaries contracted by the Venetian authorities to serve under their own leaders in squads of ten and companies of roughly 100 riders, under overall command of a Venetian *Provveditore degli Stradiotti*. The most numerous were Albanians, followed by Dalmatians and Greeks. *Stradiotti* in ancient Greek simply meant 'soldiers'; to the Venetians they were also known as *cappelletti* ('little caps') from their distinctive headgear.

Impression of a group of Venetian *stradiotti*; compare with Plate B1. None seems to wear any armour; note their Balkan headgear and (right) a quadrilateral shield and curved sabre. For many years these Albanian, Dalmatian and Greek mercenary light horse were one of Venice's major military assets.

**OPPOSITE**
Contemporary engraving of the battle of Fornovo in July 1495, with the Holy League army on the left and the French on the right. In the centre, note the French-allied Swiss pike block, above a detached group of arquebusiers, and cannon. The French artillery was prevented from firing by rain wetting its powder, and the guns were ultimately abandoned. At bottom right are French heavy cavalry *gensdarmes*; at bottom left and centre, Venetian *stradiotti* in their characteristic tall hats can be seen looting the French baggage train. This episode of ill-discipline seems to have been a turning-point in a battle in which Gonzaga's Holy League army lost twice as many men as the French, and failed to stop the French retreat out of Italy.

Mostly armed with light spears, the stradiots were among the best mounted skirmishers in the Mediterranean world: they moved fast, in any kind of terrain, and were famous for their deadly ambushes and sudden raids. They were obviously no match for heavy cavalry, so were employed mainly for reconnaissance and border patrols. They fought not only for pay but also for opportunities to loot; they were therefore prone to rioting and desertion, making it difficult to maintain discipline in their ranks, but their military value made it worth the trouble.

Initially the contracts signed by the stradiots with the republic were similar to those of the Italian mercenaries, but with the passage of time most of them passed onto the longer-term Venetian payroll. During the 16th century increasing numbers decided to move with their families into the *Terraferma*, especially to the northern region of Friuli. There, bordering the expansionist Holy Roman Empire, they settled down as soldier-colonists to keep watch over the frontier.

## REPUBLIC OF FLORENCE

The excellent Florentine citizen militia organization of the 13th century had since been abandoned. Under the Medici family in the first half of the 15th century the republic's only standing force was a 100-strong urban guard (the *fanti di Palazzo*), plus 1,000–1,500 mercenaries in 200–300 three-man 'lances' and four to six 100-man infantry companies. Nevertheless, although Florence left it late to re-acquire an effective army, the republic's great wealth would enable it to hire up to 15,000 mercenaries.

### Machiavelli's reforms

In 1505, after a decade that had seen several serious defeats, the republican government that had been restored in 1494 radically reformed its military organization along lines suggested by the famous Niccolò Machiavelli.[2]

In order to reduce the reliance on mercenaries, he sought to revive the historic republican militia, but tactically updated on the model of the latest Swiss infantry. By the end of 1505 a total of 5,000 semi-permanent militiamen had been raised throughout the areas of Tuscany that were under Florentine rule. These would be organized in companies (*gonfaloni*, 'flags'), each sub-divided into *centurie* of 100, comprising 10-man *squadre*. Led by professional officers, the companies were to muster and train 12–16 times a year. Order and discipline were to be enforced by a small number of permanent *provvisionati* – 30 mounted crossbowmen and 50 infantrymen, answering directly to the republican government. All able-bodied male citizens aged 15–50 were theoretically liable for service, but total numbers were capped at 20,000 men; those required to serve in peacetime were chosen by lot. Each *centuria* was to comprise 70 pikemen, 10 handgunners, and 20 men armed with other hand-weapons. By 1514, the Florentine militia could muster 10,000 infantrymen in 30 companies.

In 1512 Machiavelli tried to expand the new militia system to include cavalry, in order to replace the mercenary 'lances'. His original plan called for 500 horsemen armed with crossbows or handguns, grouped into ten

---

2    See Chronology. *Aide memoire*: Cosimo de' Medici the Elder gained power as 'Gran Maestro' in 1434; the Medici were exiled 1494–1512; restored 1512–27; deposed again 1527–30; restored 1530; and became Dukes of Florence in 1532.

50-man companies; unlike their infantry counterparts, these mounted militiamen were to receive regular pay. In the event, only 100 cavalrymen were recruited, and this measure remained an experiment only.

### Siege and aftermath, 1527–39

In 1527, a reorganization saw the 30 militia companies divided between two major corps with 16 and 14 companies respectively. Each division was to be commanded by a mercenary officer on a two-year contract with the republic, who was to have a personal guard of 500 mercenary infantrymen. New firearms were also purchased from Germany and distributed to the militia.

The following year, after Florence was besieged by the troops of Emperor Charles V, the militia had to be completely reorganized once again. It was now structured in two main components: the *Milizia Cittadina* or Urban Militia, with 3,000 men; and the *Milizia del Contado* or Rural Militia, with 7,000. The age limits for both categories were reduced to 18–36 in order to improve fitness. The defence of Florence during the long Imperial siege was mostly conducted by the Urban Militia, totalling 1,700 arquebusiers, 1,000 pikemen, and 300 corporals/sergeants armed with halberds. They were divided into four roughly 750-strong battalions from the city's four neighbourhoods (*Quartieri*), each sub-divided into 16 roughly 50-strong 'flags' recruited from the 64 urban districts.

After the city's fall to the Imperial siege army in 1530, and the consequent restoration of the Medici, Florence lost much of its political independence and influence; although obtaining the territories of Siena, it had to renounce any further expansionist ambitions. The republican military structures were not formally disbanded, but were deliberately neglected, while the Medici recruited a 1,000-strong mercenary force. In 1539 the Florentine militias, which had been commonly known as the *Ordinanze*, received the new denomination *Corpo delle Bande*, but their quality continued to be very low until the end of the period.

### THE PAPAL STATES

Like Florence, the Papal States lacked a solid body of militiamen or paid standing troops. However, thanks to its tax revenues from all over the Catholic world, the Papacy could afford to raise large mercenary armies at need.

### 15th century

Initially the 'lances' of the Papal cavalry had the usual three men; the man-at-arms was known as the *armigero*, the squire as the *piatto*, and the servant as the *ragazzo*. From about 1456 the Papal cavalry started to include a certain number of 'broken lances', while five-man 'cuirasses' began to appear among the 'lances' around 1463.

During the second half of the 15th century the *condotte* serving the Papacy lacked significant numbers of infantry, and the army had no independent light cavalry corps. Such infantry companies as existed

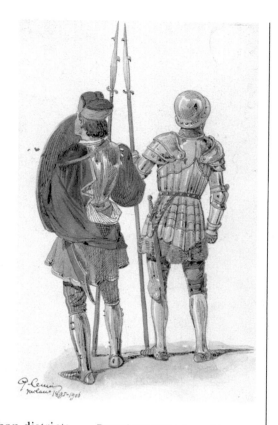

Rear-view impressions of two Italian footsoldiers of the early 16th century. (Left) seems to be a Venetian naval infantryman, protected by a full plate cuirass and greaves, and armed with a bill and a broad-bladed curved falchion sword. (Right) has a 'pot' helmet and full plate armour over ringmail; the artist has rendered the body armour in a fluted 'Gothic' style, but the large rivets at the rear of the pauldrons may be ignored.

It may be argued that the longest-lasting legacy of the Renaissance wars in Italy is the Papal Swiss Guard, still existing to this day. For the original costume, see Plate D1; this magnificent portrait of a Swiss mercenary halberdier, realized by Hans Rudolf Manuel in 1553, seems to illustrate the second version. This retained the half-blue and half-yellow livery, but with the round red cap introduced by Pope Leo X, successor to the Guard's creator Julius II. Note the two-handed sword, and, just visible slung horizontally at his right hip, a Swiss dagger.

varied widely in size according to their function, most being employed as garrisons for the many important fortifications in the territories of the Papal States. Around 1456 the first handgunners appeared in the Papal infantry companies, most being mercenaries from Germany. In 1457 the Papal field army consisted of 43 chosen 'lances' forming the personal guard of the commanding general, 400 ordinary 'lances', and 1,500 almost entirely foreign infantry. With the passage of time the infantry started to include an increasing number of *provvisionati*, who were paid on a regular basis by the *Camera Apostolica* (the Papal government). Of these, 300 chosen infantrymen acted as the pope's personal guard, and formed a significant part of Rome's garrison.

Formally, the popes could have mobilized the feudal forces of the nobility throughout the Papal territories, but these aristocrats (especially those living in Rome itself) were usually hostile rivals of the ruling pope and thus had little interest in supporting him. The capital had two distinct bodies of militia; these were of very little use in case of war, but were, in the modern sense, 'coup troops', who could apply considerable political pressure during the election of new popes. The first, the *Compagnia dei Fanti dell'Inclito Popolo Romano*, was recruited from the population of Rome, and the second, the *Milizia dei Soldati delle Battaglie del Popolo Romano*, from the rural territories of the Roman aristocracy.

### 16th century

During the early years of the century the Papal army started to be reformed, including the creation of new guard units to protect the pope. At the beginning of the century the Holy See still had a 300-strong guard, but this now consisted of one company of 200 infantrymen and a second of 100 mounted crosswbowmen. Widely hated by Rome's nobility, Pope Julius II (1503–13) lived in fear of assassination, so in 1506 he took the traditional precaution of hiring a loyal foreign bodyguard who would be immune to local factional politics. He reduced the Italian infantrymen of the Papal Guard to 100 men, but recruited a new company of 150 Swiss mercenaries. After proving its valour during the 1527 'Sack of Rome', the Swiss Papal Guard (of which this company was the nucleus) was retained by all subsequent popes.

In 1511 the Papal Guard light cavalry was divided into two independent companies; in 1531 they were reduced to a single 50-strong company; and in 1550 they were again increased to 100 men. During the first half of the century the Papal field cavalry started to have a more stable organization, in companies of 80–100 men made up from mercenary 'lances' or 'cuirasses' of traditional composition. The army also acquired some mercenary light components of Albanians, mounted crossbowmen, and German mounted arquebusiers. A certain number of Albanian stradiots, recruited with the permission of the Kings of Naples, continued to serve in the Papal army during most of the century, but were never numerous enough to become an asset on the scale of those employed by Venice.

The Papal infantry was organized into divisions called *bande*, whose strength varied from 1,200 to 5,000 men. These 'bands' were structured in companies, of strengths between 100 men and 400; four out of every five soldiers were pikemen, while the fifth had some sort of firearm. From around the mid-1500s the companies began to standardize at 200 men, and the proportion of arquebusiers was increased significantly. Most of the infantry were still mercenaries, but a certain number were long-term *provvisionati* garrison troops, stationed in fortifications and frequently performing police duties. The most important garrisons were those of the Castel Sant'Angelo in Rome, and of Ostia, the city's port. Swiss and German mercenaries remained popular, but French and Spanish also began to be employed in large numbers. From around the mid-16th century an increasing number of Papal mercenaries came from Corsica, to the point that at the beginning of the 17th century a new Corsican Guard was organized.

No general militia existed. Some of the largest Papal cities situated in the northern territory of Romagna maintained well-equipped local corps, but these were not available for Papal service except in emergencies. Finally, it is worth noting that the 16th-century Papal States could also count upon a strong fleet, outclassed only by those of Venice and Genoa.

## KINGDOM OF NAPLES

While the Kingdom of Naples was the largest regional state in Renaissance Italy, and could deploy a numerous army, several limitations had previously prevented it from becoming a great military power.

Firstly, the kingdom had few large cities, so lacked a strongly developed mercantile middle class; the majority of the population consisted of peasants living in small villages scattered across the countryside. Secondly, the kings enjoyed only nominal loyalty from a large feudal aristocracy. These *baroni* exerted complete control over most of the country, and recognized the kings' authority only formally – indeed, they spent much of their time plotting to depose the monarchs. Without their support it was practically impossible for a Neapolitan king to raise an army, and certainly not a large expeditionary force to pursue external ambitions.

In consequence, the Neapolitan kings of the early 15th century employed large numbers of *condottieri* from other areas of the peninsula, but this was not sustainable – southern Italy lacked the economic resources available to other states. Therefore, during the years 1440–60, the new Aragonese dynasty carried out a major military reform with the object of creating a powerful permanent body of heavy cavalry, to replace both the dubious feudal contingents and the former reliance on mercenary commanders.

Alfonso I, the first Aragonese King of Naples, conquered the kingdom from René of Anjou in 1442, at the head of a large mercenary force built around a core of Aragonese cavalrymen and foot crossbowmen. However, during the years that followed he tried to reduce the presence of Spanish mercenaries in order to increase his political autonomy from the Crown of Aragon. This aim was handicapped by the hostility of most of the Neapolitan nobles, who (ironically enough) still professed loyalty to the former Angevin royal family.

The territories making up the Kingdom of Naples were an administrative jigsaw puzzle, and included, dispersed among the lands of

Mercenaries gambling in their free time. The Papal States relied entirely upon mercenary armies; as well as being costly, this exposed the civil population to casual theft and drunken violence. While they were sometimes unleashed to sack enemy towns, the Landsknechts had a harsh code of discipline, enforced by sentences of death by beheading, hanging and 'running the gauntlet'. Italian *condotte* and Balkan mercenaries were less rigidly controlled, and, if their pay or rations did not arrive, the Swiss might also go marauding.

the Church and the feudal aristocracy, several domains belonging directly to the royal family. Since these were the only territories where taxes could be collected with some regularity, and whose inhabitants fulfilled their military obligations, it was to this source that Alfonso now turned. In 1450 the lands under his personal control provided few heavy knights, but Alfonso recognized that by recruiting an increasing number of 'broken lances' there he might be able to create a standing force of professional cavalrymen.

### Aragonese reforms, 1450–60s

This difficult programme was continued with more energy by Alfonso's long-lived heir, Ferrante (or Ferdinand I, r. 1458–94). As a result, by 1459 he could field about 1,000 three-man royal 'broken lances', while the feudal aristocracy could put up only 880 'lances'. Nevertheless, mercenaries contributed up to 1,200 'lances', giving the kingdom an impressive total of about 6,000 cavalrymen. (Its infantry consisted of just a few thousand mercenaries, who performed only auxiliary roles on the battlefield.) The members of the king's new 'broken lances' were known as *provvisionati demaniali*, and were provided with full equipment by the central government through the creation of a specific new tax levied throughout the kingdom.

This royal initiative was intolerable for the barons and the established *condottieri* alike, and, recognizing that a revolt was imminent, Ferdinand took a drastic decision: in 1464–65 all the 'lances' of the nobility and of the mercenary captains were pronounced 'confiscated', and absorbed into the army under royal commanders, thus bringing the entire Neapolitan cavalry into a permanent body under direct control of the king. In 1482, in time of peace, the kingdom's heavy cavalry numbered 1,200 'lances' under direct royal control and just 400 'lances' of mercenaries. Discontent naturally continued to seethe among the disempowered nobles and the largely unemployed *condottieri*; this burst out in 1485 in the great aristocratic revolt known as the *Congiura dei Baroni* (Conspiracy of the Barons), which was crushed only after hard fighting.

Until the fall of the Aragonese dynasty in 1494–96, the few infantry continued to consist of mercenaries (mostly Aragonese), and no general militia was ever organized.

### Royal guard

At the time of his arrival in Naples, Alfonso I had a strong personal guard of 1,000 men; the majority of these were Aragonese professional soldiers, commanded by their own officers. The infantrymen of the guard were divided into 28 small companies, mostly equipped as crossbowmen. With the ascendancy of Ferdinand I the Neapolitan royal guard was transformed into a cavalry force, structured in two *squadre*. The first squadron, with 25 'lances', acted as the king's mounted bodyguard; the second, with 75 'lances', was designated as the escort for the royal flags. Later in Ferdinand's reign the number of 'lances' in the royal guard was increased to 180; they were divided between five squadrons, and the previous distinction between mounted bodyguards and flag-guards was abandoned.

*(continued on page 33)*

**MILANESE ARMY**
1: Man-at-arms, 1480
2: Mounted crossbowman, 1460
3: Infantryman of *Provvisionati*, 1450s

A

**VENETIAN ARMY**
1: *Stradiotto* light cavalryman, 1500
2: '*Arsenalotto*' heavy infantryman, 1480
3: Militiaman of *Cernide*, 1515

B

**FLORENTINE ARMY**
1: Mercenary officer, 1510
2: *Fante di palazzo*, 1530
3: Arquebusier of *Milizia Cittadina*, 1530

**PAPAL ARMY**
1: Officer of Swiss Guard, 1506
2: Man-at-arms of a '*corazza*', 1470
3: Squire of a '*corazza*', 1480

**D**

**NEAPOLITAN ARMY**
1: Man-at-arms of *Provvisionati demaniali*, 1485
2: Servant of a *lancia*, 1490
3: Aragonese arquebusier, 1494

E

**FRENCH ARMY**
1: Man-at-arms of *Compagnies d'Ordonnance*, 1500
2: Archer of Scottish Guard, 1450
3: Pikeman of *Bandes Suisses*, 1478

F

**SPANISH ARMY**
1: Halberdier of *Guardia Alemana*, 1520
2: *Jinete* light cavalryman, 1500
3: *Rodelero* swordsman, 1510

**IMPERIAL ARMY**
1: Man-at-arms of 'ordnance company', 1515
2: *Reiter* pistolier light cavalryman, 1550
3: *Landsknecht Doppelsöldner*, 1528

H

# FRANCE

During most of the Hundred Years' War the French military forces had continued to be raised largely from feudal contingents. French infantry played little part, although periodically reinforced with mercenaries such as Genoese crossbowmen. Despite their excellent reputation, the French heavy cavalry had been defeated on several occasions by more balanced English armies built on strong forces of archers. Consequently, during the last years of the Hundred Years' War, King Charles VII (r. 1422–61) began to introduce reforms. The main objectives were to modernize the heavy cavalry and bring it under royal authority, and to create a professional body of infantrymen.

## Compagnies d'Ordonnance

In 1445 the best elements of the existing feudal cavalry were assembled to form a new, permanent military corps termed the *Compagnies d'Ordonnance*. These were 15 cavalry companies, one of which was to act as the king's mounted bodyguard. Each company comprised 100 'lances', but their internal structure was quite different from that of their Italian equivalents. Each comprised six fighting men: one man-at-arms, one squire (*coutilier*), one servant, and, significantly, three archers mounted for mobility. As a result, the *Compagnies d'Ordonnance* initially deployed 9,000 horsemen.

Around 1498 a fourth archer was added to each 'lance'; and later, under Francis I (r. 1515–47), a fifth archer was added, and the light cavalry *coutilier* was replaced by a second servant. In 1530 the number of 'lances' in each company was reduced to 80. In peacetime the *Compagnies d'Ordonnance* had to be maintained ready to serve, and the quality of their equipment and mounts was regularly inspected by royal officials. Thanks to the creation of this new permanent cavalry corps, on most occasions during this period French kings were freed from dependence upon inherently unreliable feudal contingents.

The success of the *Compagnies d'Ordonnance* encouraged a similar attempt to replace the previously weak and unevenly equipped feudal infantry element. The first step was to raise soldiers to garrison France's many fortresses. This new corps, known as the *Mortes-payes*, consisted of 900 dismounted four-man 'lances' each with one man-at-arms, two archers and one servant. However, the general reform of the infantry proved to be much more difficult than that of the cavalry.

## Franc-archers

In 1448, King Charles VII issued a decree that in every parish of the kingdom one archer should be chosen on the basis of his skill at arms. The chosen man, known as a *franc-archer* ('free' or 'independent archer') would be exempt from direct taxation; in exchange for this and other privileges, he had to practise shooting with the bow every Sunday, and was to hold himself ready to march with full equipment in case of royal mobilization. Many interpret this new

From his baton of command, and the heraldic quarterings on his horse's caparison, this French man-at-arms is a senior officer. The French *gensdarmes*, first assembled into permanent companies under the reforms of King Charles VII in the mid-15th century, earned an excellent reputation. During the reign of King Francis I from 1515, each tactical 'lance' comprised one man-at-arms, five foot archers and two servants, making his army a more balanced force.

**Halberdier of the Scottish Guard during the reign of Francis I.** By this date the first company of the royal guard was mostly French, and had replaced its original bows with halberds, but kept its old title. The original costume is reconstructed as Plate F2. This later version featured a slashed red hat with a white plume, and parti-coloured blue-and-red livery under a white *haqueton* embroidered with Francis's badge.

semi-permanent militia of *franc-archers* as France's first attempt to create a professional infantry corps.

Soon, however, the new troops demonstrated deficiencies on the battlefield, compared with the former example of the English and Welsh archers. They lacked training and discipline, and keeping them in good order cost the central administration a lot of money. During the reign of Louis XI (1461–83), in 1481 the *franc-archers* were temporarily disbanded; in 1485, during the reign of Charles VIII (1483–98), they were re-raised, but only to be employed as a local and purely defensive militia. Under Francis I, the corps was definitively disbanded in 1535. Organizationally, the *franc-archers* were initially grouped into companies of 200–300 men, and later into 'ensigns' of 500 archers each.

### Bandes Françaises and Swiss

From 1479, shortly before the first disbandment of the *franc-archers*, other new infantry units were organized to replace them; these were known as *Bandes Françaises*. The core of this force consisted of 10,000 veteran infantrymen and 2,500 sappers that were assembled in Picardy, where they received intensive training by instructors from among a 6,000-strong Swiss mercenary contingent hired by Louis XI in 1477. These *Bandes Suisses* were intended to form the elite of, and the model for, a new French infantry force entirely re-equipped with pikes and halberds in the Swiss manner. The Swiss returned home after a year, but the *Bandes Françaises* continued to train in Picardy for another two years, thus receiving the alternative name *Bandes de Picardie*. In 1494 a total of 4,000 infantrymen from the *Bandes Françaises* followed Charles VIII in his Italian campaign, showing their excellent quality on several occasions.

During the first half of the 16th century the new French regular infantry was constantly expanded, and was divided into two main branches: the 'Bands north of the mountains', which served in France, and the 'Bands south of the mountains', for service in Italy. The latter were also known as *Bandes de Piémont* because they were mainly based in that region of northern Italy. The *Bandes Françaises* continued to exist until 1563, when they were gradually disbanded and replaced by new 'modern' infantry regiments.

During the Italian Wars, alongside the *Bandes Françaises*, the French infantry continued to include large numbers of Swiss mercenaries; their numbers varied over time, since they were recruited according to circumstance. In 1494 there were 8,000, many of whom died during the first Italian campaign, and during the following year another 10,000 were recruited. These were all released at the end of the campaign in 1498 but in 1499 France recruited another 12,000 Swiss infantry, and 20,000 during the following year. As these numbers suggest, the Swiss were an absolutely fundamental component of the French infantry during this period.

### Royal guard

The French royal guard was officially created in 1445, when King Charles VII's first 'Company of Bodyguards' was assembled from

300 Scottish soldiers. French nobles were expressly excluded from service in the guard; as had been traditional since Classical times, hiring the best foreign mercenaries safeguarded a monarch from any treachery that might arise from local factional loyalties. The Scots were an obvious choice, since they had served for decades as allies of the French during the Hundred Years' War. The new unit was commonly known as the Scottish Guard, and initially consisted of 100 heavy armoured cavalry plus 200 foot archers, all recruited from the lesser nobility of Scotland. The 300 Scots were later divided into two companies: the 100 heavy knights who constituted the first were known as *Gentilshommes à bec-de-corbin* ('gentlemen of the crow's-beak'), from the pointed shape of their war-hammers, while the 200 foot archers of the second company became known as the 'small bodyguard'. In 1471, King Louis XI added a 100-strong company of Swiss halberdiers, the *Cent-Suisses*.

In 1474 the ranks of the royal guard were finally opened to selected French nobles, leading to the creation of another two companies. All the new French recruits had to have proved their loyalty and valour during three years' service in the army. By 1500 only the first of the 100-man guard companies was still made up of Scottish soldiers, and the following organization had been adopted (the *Cent-Suisses* also being retained separately):

The 1st Company, the Scottish Guard, included a sub-unit of 24 men who acted as the innermost bodyguard of the king, collectively known as *Gardes de la Manche* ('guards of the sleeve').

The 2nd Company, formed by French men-at-arms from the *Compagnies d'Ordonnance*, had taken over the heavy-cavalry role of the former Scottish *Gentilshommes à bec-de-corbin*.

The 3rd Company, raised in 1479, had the same characteristics as the second.

The 4th Company, organized in 1516, was created by Francis I from veterans of his former bodyguard when he was still the Dauphin.

## SPAIN

The Kingdom of Spain did not exist until 1469, when Isabel of Castile and Ferdinand of Aragon began the unification of their two kingdoms by a marriage that had enormous political importance. However, until 1492 the military forces of Castile and Aragon continued to be separate bodies, though both were heavily involved in the final decades of the *Reconquista* of southern Spain from the Moors.

As a result of the geographical and tactical character of that centuries-long war, Spanish military forces had retained certain earlier features. To fight effectively against light, mobile Moorish forces in the broken terrain of Spain, light-cavalry *jinetes* had played a larger role

The French royal guard's original Scottish heavy cavalry company was also transformed. Under Francis I it had become an infantry company of French noblemen, but retained a version of the characteristic war-hammer which had given the original '*Gentilshommes à bec-de-corbin*' their name. The hat was black with gold embroidery and white plume, and the red-and-yellow livery clothing was worn with a black cloak.

This virile figure is a member of the French royal guard's 'Cent-Suisses' company raised by King Louis XI in 1471, wearing its Germanic first costume – there was a natural intermingling between Swiss from the eastern cantons with their German neighbours. The slung hat has a layer of red feathers over a layer of white and yellow. The livery is parti-coloured yellow-and-white on his right side, and entirely red on his left. The voluminous white shirt shows under the 'slashings', which are believed to have been introduced to allow freer movement of the arms and legs in originally tight-fitting 15th-century jackets and hose.

than heavily armoured feudal knights. Consequently, when Spanish troops were on the eve of facing French heavy cavalry in Italy, the 'Catholic Monarchs' were obliged to reform their mounted units in order to acquire a permanent body of professional men-at-arms.

## Cavalry

In 1493 the Spanish heavy cavalry was reorganized as the *Guardias de Castilla*, consisting of 25 companies with 100 horsemen each. Of the 100, 75 were equipped as men-at-arms proper, and 25 as lightly equipped *jinetes*, thus unifying the two traditional elements into a single body totalling 2,500 professional horsemen. By 1506 the number of companies of Castilian Guards had been increased to 36, and most of these had already gained some combat experience in Italy. In 1525, after Spanish arquebusiers played a major part in the great Imperial victory over the French cavalry at Pavia, the *Guardias de Castilla* were reduced to just 2,000 men, distributed in 50 companies with 40 men each. (An exception was an elite 100-man company known as the *Continuos*, which continued to act as the mounted bodyguard of the Spanish king – see below.)

Generally speaking, while the Spanish heavy cavalry organized in 1493 never reached the same standards as its French counterparts, the *jinetes* were of comparable quality to the Venetian *stradiotti*. Taking as their model the Moorish troops whom they had fought for many centuries, these light horsemen were excellent hit-and-run raiders, skirmishers, and long-range scouts, capable of rapid movement over every kind of terrain. They were armed with javelins, and carried a light *adarga* shield of hardened leather in a lobed 'heart' or 'kidney' shape.

## Infantry: the *capitanía* and *coronelía*

The 1490s also saw the beginnings of the first stable organization of the Spanish infantry, already foreshadowed by Castile's employment of some Swiss instructors. Infantry were to be structured in *capitanías* or companies, each of which was divided into two *cuadrados* or squads. In 1497, during the campaign in Roussillon, three categories of infantrymen were first formally distinguished by their weapons: pikemen; *rodeleros* or *escuderos*, equipped with sword and round shield; and crossbowmen and arquebusiers – the Spanish were among the leaders in harnessing this new technology. Most infantry companies comprised roughly one-third of each of these types of soldier. The inclusion of swordsmen was not an anachronism; like the elite two-handed swordsmen among the German Landsknechts – see below – these soldiers could open gaps into the dense formations of Swiss pikemen employed by the French, as for instance at the battle of the Garigliano in October 1503.

With the Spanish intervention in the Italian Wars in the first years of the 16th century, the great Gonzalo Fernández de Córdoba gave infantry 'captaincies' a more stable organization and a fixed establishment of 500 men: 200 pikemen, 200 swordsmen and 100 arquebusiers. Ten of such

companies, plus two companies entirely of pikemen, formed a *coronelía* or 'colonelcy' totalling 6,000 soldiers. Each *coronelía* was usually deployed together with two 300-strong cavalry squadrons, one consisting of men-at-arms, the other of *jinetes*. Two *coronelías* made up an army, with 12,000 infantry and 1,200 cavalry. The 'Great Captain' Córdoba, a veteran of the last years of the *Reconquista*, employed these improved tools to fight mobile campaigns characterized by flexibility and based upon careful reconnaissance.

### The *tercio*

At some point early in the 16th century the famous term *tercio* ('third') came into use, initially to indicate each of the three pairs of *coronelías* then deployed in Italy (one pair each in Milan, Naples and Sicily). These formations later came to be known as the 'Old Tercios', to indicate their seniority.

In 1536, under the Ordinance of Genoa, *tercio* assumed a new meaning, as part of an important organizational reform. *Coronelías* began to be assembled not in pairs but in groups of three. The *coronelía* itself was reduced in size, to just four 250-man companies, thus giving the new *tercio* 12 companies (ten of pikemen and two of arquebusiers) and 3,000 men. On campaign, individual *coronelías* might be detached from their *tercios* to perform specific missions.

In addition to enjoying much greater tactical flexibility, the new *tercios* emerging from the reforms of 1536 were strictly disciplined and trained, and their qualities allowed them to dominate European battlefields for nearly a century. This, during the peak years of Spanish global superiority, instilled high morale. Exceptionally for the Renaissance period, the *tercios* already demonstrated some of the core characteristics of 'modern' infantry regiments.

### Royal guard

Initially the Spanish royal guard consisted of just one foot company with 50 halberdiers, which was organized in 1492 after a failed attempt to assassinate King Ferdinand. These *Guardias Alabarderos* were all former servants of leading Spanish noblemen; they were soon increased to 100 men, and from 1493 were supplemented by the 100 heavy cavalrymen known as *Continuos*.

In 1502 Philip of Habsburg, Archduke of Austria, visited Spain together with his personal escort of Burgundian light cavalrymen, apparently armed with bows and two-handed swords; these made a good impression in Madrid, and were thus absorbed into the Spanish royal guard as the 150-strong 'Noble Guard of Burgundian Archers'. Some time later the guard was again expanded, by the inclusion of a *stradiotti* company of 100 light-cavalry veterans of the Italian Wars. Initially these stradiots had formed the mounted bodyguard of the future King Charles's brother Ferdinand, but, like the Burgundians, they remained in Spain after a visit by their lord.

During the long years of Charles's reign as King Charles I of Spain (1516–56) and the Holy Roman Emperor Charles V (1519–56), another two companies were added. The first were 30 halberdiers known as *Guardias Viejas* ('Old Guards'), since they were all veterans from the existing guard companies who were no longer fit for active service. The other company, organized in 1519, was the *Guardia Alemana* ('German Guard') of 100 German veterans of the Imperial army; they were equipped similarly to the original Spanish *Guardias Alabarderos* but with different livery colours (see Plate G1). The Spanish royal guard thus had a distinctly international character, including chosen men from all Charles's main European Imperial dominions, but its overall strength was less than 600.

### HOLY ROMAN EMPIRE

The dominions of the Holy Roman Emperors of the Habsburg dynasty – acquired over generations by dynastic marriages and diplomacy, rather than by conquest – made up, on paper, the largest state in Europe during the Renaissance period. Essentially the legacy of the Habsburg kings of Germany, its heartland was Austria and Germany, with Hungary and

Bohemia to the east, and the Netherlands, Burgundy and Spain to the west. However, from a strictly military viewpoint the Emperor was probably the weakest monarch in Europe: in modern terms he might be described as a sort of 'chairman' or figurehead elected by his most powerful subjects, and wielding only a moral authority over their territories. Apart from troops from his personal possessions he had no standing army to speak of; he relied upon contingents from hundreds of semi-independent feudal fiefs, which ranged in size from single cities to large regional states. Each of the autonomous rulers had his own armed forces (sometimes larger than those of the Emperor), and recognized Imperial authority only formally. Emperors always had difficulty in persuading the aristocracy to wage war on external enemies distant from their own borders, so raising or funding an army involved the negotiation of political concessions and bank loans. With the Lutheran Reformation of the early 16th century, even the Emperor's moral authority began to disappear: he remained a Roman Catholic, while, in time, a majority of the German princes became Protestants.

During the 16th-century wars the Holy Roman Emperors were Maximilian I (r. 1493–1519), and his grandson Charles V (r. 1519–56). Since Maximilian had had the foresight to marry two of his children to two potential heirs to the Spanish throne, Charles V was simultaneously King Charles I of Spain, which would enable him to employ excellent Spanish *tercios* to crush rebellious German Protestant princes. He could never create a German standing army, but he was able to deploy large numbers of German mercenary soldiers in the Italian peninsula – *Landsknechte* infantry and *Reiter* cavalry.

A member of the Spanish *Guardias Alabarderos* company in the late costume adopted after the abdication of Charles V in 1556. The red cap has plumes in red, yellow and white. The coat and trousers are basically yellow, under chequered stripes of red and white. For the company's earlier uniform, see page 45.

## Infantry

The term *Landsknechte* ('servants of the land') seems to have been used first in the 1470s, of mercenaries hired by Charles the Bold, Duke of Burgundy (r. 1467–77); by 1500 it was sometimes corrupted into *Lanzknechte* ('servants of the pike'). Maximilian I first hired them as part his efforts to professionalize the troops available to him, learning

A German engraving emphasizing the flamboyant Landsknecht costume, worn by (left to right) a swordsman, a fifer, a drummer, an ensign with a flag and a ringmail cape, and a *Trabant* halberdier bodyguard. In Landsknecht units the fifer and drummer stayed close to their ensign; drumbeats indicated the pace of the march, speeding up to encourage an advance on the battlefield.

**ABOVE LEFT**
Contemporary German print showing Landsknecht pikemen in slashed and (left) parti-coloured clothing; the depiction of the looter (right) emphasizes the width of the unfolded hat, slashed at the brim. The ringmail cape protecting the shoulders and upper torso seems to have been popular among these troops. Note also their almost universal sidearm, the short '*katzbalger*' sword with S-shaped quillons.

**ABOVE RIGHT**
Apparently from the same source as the previous pikeman print, this engraving shows a halberd-armed *Weibel* (non-commissioned officer) named as Ulrich von Zalm Parchant Weber. The slashing and bunching of the hose differs from one leg to the other.

from crushing defeats suffered by Burgundy in its wars against the Swiss during the late 1470s. His aim was to create German infantry of a quality comparable to the then apparently invincible Swiss pikemen, since the latter would be hired in large numbers by Maximilian's rival, Louis XI of France.

In about 1486 the first 8,000-odd German mercenaries were assembled by Maximilian for campaigns in the Low Countries and Bohemia, and from 1490 they began to acquire a reputation for good training and discipline. Thereafter, the Landsknechts were organized into regiments recruited on the basic model of the Italian *condotte*. A *Kriegsherr* ('gentleman of war'), often a minor noble or the younger son of an aristocratic family, sought from the Emperor 'letters patent' that named him an *Obrist* ('colonel') instructed to raise a unit. Funding might be by a direct grant from the Emperor, or a loan provided by an important banker acting on his behalf. (As the wars ground on, it was sometimes late in coming; in 1526 the great Landsknecht general Georg von Frundsberg had to fund the raising of a large corps out of his own pocket.)

The strengths of units naturally varied over time and circumstance, but the following establishment of an early 16th-century regiment is recorded in documents of the Imperial administration. Soldiers were usually hired for six months' service – a single campaign season. A regiment was structured in ten *Fahnlein* ('flags') or companies, each of 400 men led by a captain with two junior officers; in newly recruited regiments, colonels tried to include at least 100 veterans in each company. A company comprised 40 *Rotten* or platoons of ten men (or six *Doppelsöldner* – see below), each led by a *Rottmeister* (roughly, a corporal) elected by his own soldiers. Liaison between the rankers and officers (an interestingly modern idea) was the job of a *Gemeinweibel*, a spokesman who was rotated monthly by election. The 400 'NCOs' in the 4,000-man regiment were responsible for basic training and discipline, under the supervision of *Feldweibel* (roughly, sergeants), and a regimental *Oberster-Feldweibel* responsible for the formation for battle. Each colonel commanding in the field (*Feldobrist*) had a personal staff including subordinate officers and a chaplain, scribe, interpreter, scout, doctor, quartermaster, ensign, drummer, fifer and eight *Trabanten* bodyguards. Discipline was strictly enforced at regimental level by a provost, whose retinue included an executioner. Although naturally vulnerable under campaign conditions, on paper the whole contractual and administrative apparatus was impressively comprehensive.

The 400 men of a company were supposed to be equipped 300 with pikes, 50 with two-handed swords or halberds, and 50 with arquebuses. The swordsmen/halberdiers and arquebusiers, who needed initiative and boldness above that of the massed ranks of pikemen, were volunteers chosen for their qualities and rewarded with double-pay, thus being termed *Doppelsöldner*.

Landsknecht tactics were not dissimilar to those of the Swiss they often faced, but proved more flexible, since (as in the Spanish *tercio*) the number of arquebusiers increased over time, and two-handed swordsmen and halberdiers were deployed to cut paths into a solid enemy pike block. A Landsknecht regiment was drawn up in a pike square, but with the first two ranks composed of *Doppelsöldner*; if the latter succeeded in breaking the integrity of the enemy front ranks, the compact mass of pikemen pushed forward to exploit the gaps. Usually the most experienced pikemen and halberdiers were placed in the rear ranks, to maintain order in the formation and prevent flight. The arquebusiers were deployed all round the flanks of the square to protect it from cavalry charges; from the mid-16th century it became common for the more numerous arquebusiers to form four wings, firing and falling back in turn to support an advance.

**Landsknecht *Doppelsöldner* with two-handed sword (see also Plate H3); he wears almost full armour, due to his exposed position in the front or rear ranks of a pike square, and his mission in battle. Half of the 100 *Doppelsöldnern* in a 400-man company formation were usually armed with this *zweihander* and/or halberds, the other half with arquebuses.**

Impression of a mid-16th century German *Reiter* light horseman, wearing a popular burgonet helmet and what seems to be half-armour with a breastplate only. He has two wheel-lock pistols, one tucked in his belt and the other in its saddle-holster; these first appeared during the 1540s. Given the complexity of the wheel-lock system, and the consequent high cost of the pistols to employers, we may assume that such 'pistoliers' must have proved their value in battle.

In this impression the Imperial light cavalryman carries both the light spear with which these mercenaries were originally provided, and a pair of saddle-pistols. He wears no armour, but has a 'combed morion' helmet. The trumpeter's hat has a Balkan look, but the source for the rest of his costume is a mystery.

On several occasions the Landsknechts did indeed defeat the Swiss, as, famously, at Marignano (1515). As parts of the multinational armies of the shifting alliances that characterized the Italian Wars, they became the most famous and effective mercenaries in Europe. While they would form the core of Imperial armies, they also hired themselves out to other powers, even to fight against the Empire. For instance, in 1515 Francis I of France employed a German mercenary corps of up to 17,000 infantry (12,000 pikemen, 2,000 swordsmen, 1,000 halberdiers and 2,000 arquebusiers). A typical later example of a battle between multinational forces was that of Scannagallo in August 1554, between Sienese-French and Florentine-Imperial armies. For Siena, the *condottiero* Piero Strozzi commanded about 5,000 Italians, 4,000 French, 3,000 Landsknechts and 3,000 Swiss, while Gian Giacomo Medici's Florentine army consisted of perhaps 7,500 Italians and Balkan mercenaries, 4,000 Landsknechts, and 4,000 Spanish.

## Cavalry

Influenced by the contemporary French 'ordnance companies', in 1477 Maximilian I decided to organize his own permanent heavy cavalry by retaining in service four of the 12 Burgundian *Compagnies d'Ordonnance* that had been created by Charles the Bold. Upon Charles's death in battle that year, at the hands of the Swiss at Nancy, Maximilian had inherited the Duchy of Burgundy by virtue of being married to the dead duke's daughter (although he soon lost it, after an unlucky war against France).

Each cavalry company comprised 20 five-man 'lances' in the French style, so the four companies deployed a total of 100 men-at-arms, who made up the Emperor's personal escort. Maximilian's successor Charles V doubled the number of companies in 1522, and expanded them to 15 during the years 1545–47. On that occasion, however, the number of 'lances' in a company was halved to 10; and since the original Burgundian structure has been abandoned, the resultant 50-man companies were entirely composed of heavy men-at-arms.

Since his accession in 1519, Charles V had also begun to develop a new category of German mercenary cavalry, hired on much the same lines as the Landsknecht infantry, and these 'riders' (*Reiter*) would come to form the bulk of the Imperial cavalry during the Renaissance period.

They were lightly armoured horsemen riding unarmoured horses; initially their primary weapon was the 'boar-spear', but by the mid-16th century an increasing number of them had started to be equipped as 'pistoliers' with a pair of wheel-lock pistols. If they had any armour at all it might be very light, consisting of partial ringmail protection; this allowed them to operate in a way comparable to the Venetian *stradiotti* or the Spanish *jinetes*. The basic unit was the squadron, usually numbering 300 men. The pistoliers employed the cavalry tactic known as the 'caracole', whereby they advanced in successive ranks to discharge their pistols at very close range, before withdrawing to the rear of the squadron to reload, each rank then moving forward again in its turn.

# SELECT BIBLIOGRAPHY

Artusi L., & Semplici, R., *Il Corteo della Repubblica Fiorentina* (Scramasax, 2011)

Bueno, José Maria, *Guardias Reales de España* (Aldaba Militaria, 1989)

Covini, Maria Nadia, *L'esercito del Duca: organizzazione militare e istituzioni al tempo degli Sforza, 1450–1480* (Istituto Storico Italiano per il Medioevo, 1998)

Delabos, C. & Gaillard, P., *Montlhéry, 16 juillet 1465* (Historic'One Editions, 2003)

Giorgetti, Niccolò, *Le Armi Toscane e le occupazioni straniere in Toscana, 1537–1860* (Ufficio Storico dello Stato Maggiore dell'Esercito, 1916)

Gush, George, *Renaissance Armies, 1480–1650* (Patrick Stephens Ltd, 1975)

Heath, Ian, *Armies of the Middle Ages*, Vols 1 & 2 (Wargames Research Group, 1982 & 1984)

Michael, N. & Embleton, G., *Armies of Medieval Burgundy, 1364–77*, MAA 144 (Osprey Publishing, 1983)

Miller, D. & Embleton, G., *The Landsknechts*, MAA 58 (Osprey Publishing, 1976)

Miller, D. & Embleton, G., *The Swiss at War, 1300–1500*, MAA 94 (Osprey Publishing, 1979)

Murphy, David, *Condottiere, 1300–1500*, Warrior 115 (Osprey Publishing, 2007)

Nicolle, David, *Italian Medieval Armies, 1300–1500*, MAA 136 (Osprey Publishing, 1983)

Nicolle, David, *The Venetian Empire, 1200–1670*, MAA 210 (Osprey Publishing, 1989)

Notario López, Ignacio & Iván, *The Spanish Tercios, 1536–1704*, MAA 481 (Osprey Publishing, 2012)

Pohl, John M.D. & Embleton, G., *Armies of Castile & Aragon, 1370–1516*, MAA 500 (Osprey Publishing, 2015)

Predonzani, Massimo, *Ceresole, 1544* (Historic'One Editions, 2012)

Richards, John, *Landsknecht Soldier, 1486–1560*, Warrior 49 (Osprey Publishing, 2002)

Storti, Francesco, *L'Esercito Napoletano nella seconda metà del Quattrocento* (Laveglia Editore, 2007)

Susane, Louis Auguste, *Histoire de l'Infanterie Française* (Librairie Corréard, 1849)

Susane, Louis Auguste, *Histoire de la Cavalerie Française* (Librairie Hetzel, 1874)

# PLATE COMMENTARIES

## A: MILANESE ARMY
### A1: Man-at-arms, 1480
From the late 14th century the armouries of Milan produced the best plate armour in Europe; it was about 1420 before their south German counterparts began to rival them with distinctively fluted 'Gothic' armours. Milanese armours, with a rather plain, rounded, functional appearance, were used by the majority of Italian knights throughout the Renaissance period. The helmet here is a visored sallet, worn above a deep bevor and gorget. When not in battle helmets were replaced by two types of headgear, both termed the *beretta*: a stiff, cylindrical type made in felt, or a softer cap made of wool. There was no visible difference between the gear of knights serving in a *lancia* or in a *lancia spezzata*.

### A2: Mounted crossbowman, 1460
The Milanese mounted crossbowmen, employed mainly to patrol the countryside and frontiers, were true cavalrymen, in that they could use their weapons from the saddle. Their equipment comprised a *celata* (sallet) helmet, a gorget, and a *panziera* cuirass (or perhaps a breastplate alone). Mounted crossbowmen became popular in Italy as bodyguards after the Swiss fielded them as advance scouts, though the latter dismounted to fight.

A French heavy cavalryman from the *Compagnies d'Ordonnance*; the Germanic appearance of his armour probably dates him to about 1540, although 'Gothic' armours had apparently been popular among the original Burgundian companies of the 1470–80s.

This soldier carries a horn, which was used to communicate during both reconnaissance missions and battles.

### A3: Infantryman of the *provvisionati*, 1450s
This soldier on the duchy's regular payroll is one of the chosen infantrymen who made up the urban guard of Milan. His painted *barbuta* helmet is worn together with a padded *gambeson*. As was common in this period, plate armour is worn only on his left leg, which was advanced in combat below his shield. The latter bears the coat-of-arms of the Sforza family, the *condottieri* who became rulers of Milan from 1450. His main weapon is a bill, a popular polearm among Italian infantry of the early Renaissance.

## B: VENETIAN ARMY
### B1: *Stradiotto* light cavalryman, 1500
The distinctive equipment of the Balkan *stradiotti* was characteristic of the Albanian and Greek regions where they were recruited. Over time, this cylindrical black felt hat was replaced by soft round caps in various colours, from which these mercenary light cavalry got their alternative nickname of '*capelletti*'. They seldom wore any metal armour, except sometimes elements of ringmail, and relied upon padded fabric protection. Their primary weapons were light spears known (strikingly, to modern ears) as *assegai*, but they might also carry composite bows; secondary weapons included curved sabres, small axes or maces. Note the characteristic 'swept quadrilateral' shape of the Balkan shield.

### B2: '*Arsenalotto*' heavy infantryman, 1480
The 630 chosen infantrymen who made up the urban guard of Venice were also workers in the city's famous Arsenal, hence their popular name. Since they were equipped as heavy infantrymen, their overall appearance was similar to that of the ordinary militiamen chosen for active service on Venetian warships. The sallet helmet is worn together with a brigandine corselet reinforced internally with small metal plates, over a long-sleeved ringmail shirt. The oval shield bears the blazon of St Mark, the traditional protector of Venice. His main weapon is a deadly war-hammer, which was also popular among Venetian naval infantrymen.

### B3: Militiaman of the *Cernide*, 1515
Significant numbers of these local militiamen were equipped as handgunners from their first raising, and in many ways they were superior to other militias organized by Italian states during the period. Most Venetian infantry ceased to receive armour from the early years of the 16th century. The everyday clothes of Renaissance Italy were characterized by bright colours and 'slashings', as represented here – this was by no means only a German fashion. The *daga* sidearm was characteristic of all Venetian infantrymen.

## C: FLORENTINE ARMY
### C1: Mercenary officer, 1510
Before Machiavelli's reforms the Florentine army was entirely made up of mercenaries, commanded by *condottieri* like the man represented here. Most of them were wealthy enough to buy the best personal equipment available at the time, such as this *borgonotto* (burgonet) helmet and plate half-armour. White and red were the colours of Florence, and this officer's status is shown by the red sash worn from shoulder to hip.

### C2: *Fante di palazzo*, 1530

The fanti di palazzo both provided the personal guard of the Medici family, and garrisoned the most important public buildings in Florence. They were equipped as heavy infantrymen, with gorget and panziera worn over a protective leather jerkin. The clothing is in the distinctive colours of the Florentine Republic, and the soft round hat is fashionably decorated with three feathers. The main weapon is a pike, carried together with a sword.

### C3: Arquebusier of the *Milizia Cittadina*, 1530

The infantry militia created by Machiavelli from 1505 originally had only ten arquebusiers in each 100-man *centuria*, but as the years passed the proportion increased steadily. There was no standardization of the firearms used in Italy, and arquebuses were bought from various sources, mostly German or Spanish. The weapon illustrated is of a very up-to-date shape, although wooden shoulderstocks had been in use since at least the 1480s. All arquebuses were matchlocks; since at least 1411, the match had been held in a 'serpentine' clamp activated by a trigger bar or button. The militiaman illustrated is better dressed and equipped than was the norm, but the *Ordinanze* included men of various social classes. In this case the puffed and slashed trousers are not dissimilar from those of the German Landsknechte, who by this date were familiar figures all over Italy. The 'combed morion' helmet is today popularly associated with the Spanish, but was in fact first produced in Italy.

### D: PAPAL ARMY

### D1: Officer of the Swiss Guard, 1506

According to tradition, the first 'uniform' of the Papal Swiss Guard was designed by Michelangelo himself; when the corps was created the artist was in fact in Rome, in the employment of Pope Julius II, whose distinctive yellow-and-blue livery colours were used by his new Guard. On active service helmets and half-armour were worn, but otherwise soft caps like this example were popular, as confirmed in a famous painting by Raphael from which this early costume is reconstructed. Halberds were carried by the soldiers and 'NCOs', while officers were armed only with a sword.

### D2: Man-at-arms of a *'corazza'*, 1470

From 1463 the Papal 'lances' started to have five members instead of three, and assumed the new denomination of 'cuirasses'. The Papal heavy men-at-arms were all mercenaries, coming from several areas of Italy; but their personal equipment was quite uniform, since it usually comprised Milanese plate armour of the kind illustrated. 'Close helmets' were frequently decorated with coloured

feathers, similar to those worn during tournaments. The heraldic arms and livery colours of each knight might be reproduced on the *bardatura* of his warhorse.

### D3: Squire of a *'corazza'*, 1480

The second member of each tactical 'lance' or 'cuirass' had different denominations in the various Italian states; in the Papal army he was known as the *piatto*. These squires were all equipped as light cavalrymen, and rode unarmoured horses. Here, a simple breastplate is worn together with a *barbuta* helmet, and high leather boots typical of light cavalry of the period. Weaponry consisted of a cavalry spear and a sword; here, he carries another lance for the man-at-arms commanding his sub-unit, which flies a small flag showing the knight's heraldry.

**ABOVE LEFT**

Impression of a Spanish royal guardsman of the *Guardias Alabarderos* company in the first costume introduced in 1492. The black hat has a white plume, and the parti-coloured surcoat is in red and white, with trim in the opposite colours.

**ABOVE RIGHT**

A member of the *Guardias Alabarderos* during the reign of Charles V. The hat is in the same colours, but the Germanic-looking 16th-century costume is now in yellow and red. Note the change in fashion from long hair and a clean-shaven face to short hair and a beard; this was copied elsewhere in the Empire.

## E: NEAPOLITAN ARMY

### E1: Man-at-arms of the *provvisionati demaniali*, 1485
Following the reforms of the Aragonese monarchs Alfonso I and Ferrante I in the mid-15th century, the Kingdom of Naples had the best heavy cavalry in Italy. All Neapolitan men-at-arms, be they royal or feudal, had the same kind of personal equipment, comprising a full set of Milanese plate armour as well as heavy horse-armour. Individual wealth was indicated by the degree and complexity of the additional decoration.

### E2: Servant of a *lancia*, 1490
During the Renaissance period the only Neapolitan infantry consisted of the servants from the 'lances' and mercenary infantrymen, who were a minor component of the *condotte* in the service of the Aragonese kings. Some of these wore helmets and partial armour, but the majority were unarmoured. As throughout Renaissance Italy, Neapolitan clothing was colourful and richly decorated; it was worn with small caps, white shirts, and *brache* (hose) sometimes parti-coloured. This soldier carries an early form of partizan, a broad-headed weapon that could be particularly effective against the mounts of cavalrymen.

### E3: Aragonese arquebusier, 1494
Firearms never became particularly popular among Italians, because the *condottieri* were slow to adopt new military technology. Consequently, the arquebusiers found in the Italian armies of the early Renaissance were usually German

mercenaries, but the best crossbowmen and handgunners were mostly Aragonese. This man carries measured powder charges in an early example of the 'Eleven Apostles' (small tubular flasks strung to a crossbelt), spare or finer priming powder in a horn, and balls in a leather pouch. At the turn of the 16th century arquebuses were only effective against plate armour at very short ranges, but they were deadly for horses and unarmoured infantrymen. Longer, heavier matchlock 'muskets', usually fired from a forked rest, began to appear in about the 1520s.

In the 1490s the Spanish '*Gran Capitán*', Gonzalo Fernández de Córdoba, who was sent to support the Neapolitans, was hampered by their conservative attitudes. When given freedom to operate, in 1503 he famously deployed his arquebusiers – 20 per cent of his infantry – to great effect at Cerignola, where they lined a defensive trench on a slope, protected by stakes, and decimated the French cavalry who charged right up to their position.

## F: FRENCH ARMY

### F1: Man-at-arms of *Compagnies d'Ordonnance*, 1500
At the outbreak of the Italian Wars – some 80 years after their defeats at the hands of the English during the Hundred Years' War – the French men-at-arms (literally known as *gensdarmes*) were considered to be the best heavy cavalry in Europe. As throughout much of the continent, Milanese plate armour was popular in France, and could be found much more frequently than its 'Gothic' equivalent, which was in widespread use only in the Duchy of Burgundy. The 'close helmet' or armet had now replaced the previous sallet-and-bevor combination. Over a generation during the Italian Wars, from Cerignola in 1503 to Pavia in 1525, it became apparent that the 'glory days' of the French heavy cavalry were over: pike blocks, field cannon, arquebuses, and more mobile light horsemen gradually degraded the supremacy of the *gensdarmes*.

### F2: Archer of the Scottish Guard, 1450
The first 'uniform' provided for the 200 foot archers of the Scottish Guard was a *haqueton* in the green, white and red colours of King Charles VII's livery, as also seen in the decorative feather plume attached to the visored sallet helmet. The white embroidery represents Charles's distinctive badge of rose-stalks, under a royal crown. Under his livery this minor Scottish nobleman has full plate armour. His main weapon is a longbow, carried together with a sword and a small buckler for self-defence. The *franc-archers* were equipped quite similarly, though obviously without the Guard's distinctions.

### F3: Pikeman of the *Bandes Suisses*, 1478
The many Swiss mercenaries serving in French armies varied considerably in their equipment: those who fought in the front ranks wore sallet or *cervelière* helmets and extensive plate armour, even down to below the knee, while the rank-and-file might wear Swiss turban headgear, and ringmail shirts under their outer clothing. The poorest and most recent recruits simply wore their everyday clothes – perhaps, as here, in cantonal colours, though these were not displayed in any systematic way (white and red were not limited to the canton of Berne). The white cross sewn to his sleeve and hose was first recorded as the Swiss field-sign in 1339. In addition to the 16-foot pike, he is armed with a typical *Schweizergegen* shortsword/long dagger on his right side, and in this case has also acquired a French or Italian hand-and-a-half sword.

**Landsknechts: the arquebusier (left) interestingly wears a breastplate, faulds and tassets, reminding us that these men made up about half of a company's *Doppelsöldnern*. The ensign (second left) has the familiar ringmail cape.**

## G: SPANISH ARMY

### G1: Halberdier of the *Guardia Alemana*, 1520

The German halberdiers of the Spanish royal guard wore this distinctive livery in yellow and white, and were commonly known as *Guardias Blancas*, to distinguish them from the company of Spanish halberdiers dressed in red and yellow (*Guardias Amarillas*). The guard heavy cavalry of the *Continuos* wore complete Milanese plate armour, but could be recognized by the Castilian coat-of-arms on the horses' caparisons. The Burgundian horse-archers wore a *haqueton* surcoat with the coat-of-arms of their duchy.

### G2: *Jinete* light cavalryman, 1500

The Spanish light cavalry wore a mix of Spanish and Moorish elements. The sallet helmet with eye-slots, and the breastplate, are clearly Spanish, while the javelins and the *adarga* shield are typical of Muslim mounted troops from Andalucía. The light shield, of characteristic lobed shape, was made of hardened leather, which was sufficient to protect the *jinete* from the arrows and javelins of enemy skirmishers.

### G3: *Rodelero* swordsman, 1510

Before the great reform of the *tercios* ordered in 1536, the Spanish infantry 'captaincies' comprised three categories of soldiers: pikemen, swordsmen and crossbowmen/handgunners. The *rodeleros* or *escuderos* derived their name from the *rodela* or round shield, with a central spike that had offensive value in hand-to-hand combat. Like the Landsknecht *Doppelsöldner* with a two-handed sword (see Plate H3), this soldier's task was to cut the pikeshafts of the enemy's front ranks. This might seem a suicide mission, but the 16-foot pike was an unwieldy weapon, and pikemen were vulnerable once a more agile man got between the points and up to close quarters. The excellent Spanish swords, produced in Toledo, were the best in Europe. The red St Andrew's Cross, here painted on the breastplate, was distinctive of Spanish armies during the Renaissance (as it had previously been of the Duchy of Burgundy).

## H: IMPERIAL ARMY

### H1: Man-at-arms of an 'ordnance company', 1515

This personal retainer of the Emperor Maximilian I serves in one of the four *Compagnies d'Ordonnance* which he inherited from Charles the Bold of Burgundy following the latter's death in 1477. He wears an example of so-called 'Maximilian' armour; a more rounded-looking evolution of the late 15th-century German 'High Gothic' style, it lacks its predecessor's pointed details, but retains the radial fluting which strengthened thinner and therefore lighter plates. It is misleading to try to identify armour styles too closely with areas of manufacture; effective designs naturally became popular, and were widely traded and copied. Milanese armours were certainly worn in the Empire; and one German armour made for Maximilian himself, apparently in Augsburg, lacks any fluting, but instead has dozens of ventilation slots in the visor and gauntlets.

### H2: *Reiter* pistolier, 1550

By the mid-16th century German light cavalry were among the most successful mercenaries in Europe, being employed in several armies outside the Empire. Such horsemen usually wore only light protection – in this case a 'combed morion', and a ringmail cape. In addition to his sword, this *Reiter* carries a pair of wheel-lock pistols holstered on his saddle, which have replaced his original light spear as his primary weapons.

### H3: *Landsknecht Doppelsöldner*, 1528

Unlike the ordinary pikemen, who seldom had any armour beyond a ringmail shoulder-cape, the 'double-pay soldiers' who were exposed to hand-to-hand combat wore cuirasses or half-armour (though backplates were scorned, since a true fighting man never turned his back on the enemy). The large plumed hats, and loose parti-coloured clothing decorated with slashings revealing the white shirt, were common to all Landsknechts. Colours were random; the only known example of 'uniform' were the slashed red jackets and trousers provided for his regiment in 1529 by the Nuremberg aristocrat Willibald Pirkheimer. The short *katzbalger* sword with an S-shaped guard was almost universal, but the long, double-edged *zweihander*, used to cut off enemy pikeheads, was particular to the *Doppelsöldner*. The chosen *Trabanten* of a colonel's bodyguard might be equipped similarly to this figure, but carried halberds.

An interesting, if puzzling, impression of a 16th-century *Reiter* and his officer. The half-armoured trooper carries a wheel-lock pistol at his hip, a rondel dagger behind his waist, and – unusually for a light horseman? – an arquebus. The officer is distinguished by his sash, more complete armour with large pauldrons, and more elaborate costume: slashed and ribboned 'upper stocks', and what are drawn as short ringmail boots with leather soles.

# INDEX